KAILA YU AND KIKI WONG

30-Day Travel Challenge

How to Make Your Travel Dreams a Reality

Contents

III Week 3: Taking actionable steps

IV Week 4: Crossing the finish line

Introduction

Wanderlust—a term that's been resonating throughout the current social lingo and media outlets. It's the ultimate desire held by many, but followed through and experienced by few. So many people worldwide share this dream of travel, but most people have no knowledge or resources to make their dreams come to life.

However, the amount of Americans leaving the US is now booming. In 2016, a total of 66,960,943 U.S. citizens explored the world beyond our borders. That's a whopping 8% increase from the previous year!

Social media outlets have been saturated with eye-catching and jaw-dropping images of bloggers on their glorious destinations abroad, making it even more tantalizing to those with a serious case of the travel bug.

But, many suffer from beliefs that are holding them back:
Traveling is too expensive ...
Traveling is too difficult ...
Traveling is too confusing ...

So, how exactly do THEY do it?

JOIN THE 30-DAY TRAVEL CHALLENGE!

We are Kaila and Kiki.

We are frequent travelers.

With a combined social media reach of 2.5 million+, we've been fortunate enough to share our travel experiences with fellow travel enthusiasts, and even get paid to travel the world.

Neither of us are trust fund babies.

We don't have millions of dollars.

We are not flight attendants.

All we had was the undying feeling of wanderlust, and we had to do something to appease it.

As small children, we both were lucky enough to have travel infused in our lives at an early age, from each of our families. Kaila's parents are from Taipei, Taiwan, so she frequently traveled back to Taipei every few years to visit all of our relatives. Her family would also often take road trips within driving distance from Kiki's home in Southern California while growing up.

Kiki's family instilled the value of travel and building experiences like an engraving in stone. Her parents insisted that money should be spent on extraordinary adventures and life experiences, rather than materialistic values. This led to a healthy resume of travels, and a passionate desire to travel more.

As we both reached adulthood, we both found careers in our early twenties that allowed plenty of travel. However, those careers ended rather abruptly and we went through a period where we could no longer afford to travel, because we were dirt broke!

While working hard to build another thriving career, we followed bloggers and travel writers who were living out our dreams. Living vicariously through these professional travelers, we soaked up everything that we could possibly learn and reinvented ourselves in a new career as a travel writers/bloggers.

You don't need to become a travel writer to travel more, but you can definitely incorporate many of the tips and tricks that travel bloggers and writers regularly use to enable you to travel much more frequently.

One of the greatest and most humbling things about being in the public eye on social media is the comments and feedback from our followers. Most of the time, people say, "You have a dream job," and "I wish that I could travel as much as you do!"

While interacting with our readers, we've found so many people believe that travel is unattainable and entirely cost-prohibitive.

This is simply **not** true.

And so, we wanted to write this book and create this challenge to show you that travel **IS** possible. Most importantly, we want to provide an actionable, step-by-step program to unveil more travel experiences into your life.

So, why should you travel?

Exploring the world gives you a new perspective on life. It allows people to experience, first-hand, new cultures, customs, and worlds other than their own.

Seeing the world helps you break out of your daily routine, what you know best, those clockwork days. Also, getting to know people outside of your immediate circles can help expand the way you think and elevate your creativity.

Travel also challenges you. It gets you out of your comfort zone and exercises skills that you would have never developed just by sitting at home. Whether you are testing your culinary skills in a cooking class in the south of France or exploring the magnificent ruins of Machu Picchu in Peru, these new experiences will often instill an indescribable change in you that will give you ultimate fulfillment.

Are you in?

Good!

Brace yourself, because you are going to embark on an exciting journey this month! For these next 30 days, travel will be the main focus of your life, something that you've probably never done before. It will be a time of great self-reflection, stepping beyond the boundaries of your comfort zone, and kickstarting some serious electrical signals to parts of your brain that may have been dormant. Basically, we'll be kicking your brain's butt in the best way possible!

You WILL achieve more travel this next year, as long as you fully **commit** to this challenge.

Without further ado, let's GO!

How does it work?

In this challenge, we'll be working together as a team to finish this 30-day course.

In the first week, we'll start off by assessing where you are in your travel beliefs and current traveling status—you may be surprised to discover the subconscious thoughts that might be holding you back from your travel dreams.

We'll set a foundation of healthy practices to help supercharge this challenge by exploring tools such as meditation and journaling.

We'll end the week with some motivationally stimulating activities, such as deciding where you want to travel to next and exploring your hometown. We're going to get you traveling immediately—don't worry! (Traveling locally in your hometown counts).

Here's what we've got planned for you:

Week 1: Setting the foundation

We will tackle the deep process of self-reflection and exploration. We'll introduce several actions which you might enjoy enough to incorporate them as permanent, daily practices in your life.

During this first week, we'll also explore some of your dream destinations and pick at least one of these that you would like to visit next.

Week 2: Finding inspiration

Inspiration can be found almost anywhere. We'll go step-by-step and discover the ways in which you can motivate yourself to take the necessary steps towards traveling more.

You'll reach out to other travelers and build your own travel community. We'll even guide you on how to start a travel fund, allowing you to see more places beyond your imagined budget.

Week 3: Taking actionable steps

By now, you'll have set the foundation in Week 1 and received tons of inspiration in Week 2.

Now that you're at the halfway point of the challenge, we're going to actually plan your dream trip, and set up a working budget and a savings plan. We'll even explore ideas on how to kickstart your travel fund, set achievable goals, learn all about travel-hacking, and explore travel credit cards.

We weren't kidding about the actionable steps this week; you'll be a giant step closer to your dream trip!

Week 4: Crossing the finish line

By now, you'll be a travel-planning superstar!

In Week 4, we have some fun activities; like creating your bucket list and planning a weekend getaway (or staycation). There's still a bit more work to do, such as exploring alternative accommodation to save money and looking into travel hacks to find cheap flights. But don't worry, it's a far lighter load than Week 3!

Each week also includes a day of rest. On the last day of each week, we'll be spending a bit of time reviewing the previous week's work and reflecting on what we have learned. This is an important step of the process in order to create lasting change, so don't skip out on spending just a little bit of time on your rest day to reflect on your previous week.

After the challenge

At the end of the challenge, we'll explore ideas on how to keep the motivation going after the challenge is over. The point of this challenge is to make a permanent lifestyle change. By the end of the challenge, the vital tools you've learned can be applied to all walks of life. Use them!

If you're feeling overwhelmed at tackling this solo, you're not in this challenge alone. We highly encourage you to connect with the 30-Day Travel Challenge community by posting your photos of your personal journey on Facebook, Twitter, Instagram or whichever platform you love the most, using the challenge hashtag **#30DaysToTravel**.

Also, we have set up a <u>Facebook group</u> for daily inspiration and support from others who are also taking the 30 Day Travel Challenge. Make sure to come and say hello!

Get your highlighter out, your page tabs ready, and your mind open because we're about to go in ... 3 ... 2 ...1 ...

I

Week 1: Setting the foundation

1

Day 1: Let's get started!

Today's challenge: Commit to this journey!

There's nothing better than a challenge!

In the past, we've taken on several of our own 30-day challenges.

Here are a few of our endeavors: A commitment to meditate for once a month with guided meditations, a 30-day blog challenge, 30-day exercise plans, and more.

These types of challenges allow you to create tangibility to goals by setting a timeline and recording your daily progress.

It also really helps to tackle challenges with friends. Many years ago, Kaila and one of her friends worked through the challenge book *Life Makeovers* by Cheryl Richardson. It took a full year for them to complete all the actions in the book. Ultimately, they finished it because they had both made a commitment to each other to see it through to the end.

Having a challenge buddy can make the process so much more fun and rewarding. But if you are taking the challenge by yourself, do not fear. We've done tons of challenges by ourselves and they are just as effective.

Remember, we are in this together, so you can always reach out to us for love and support. Send us a message on our blogs, social media accounts, or even email! We'd love to help you through your challenge each step of the way.

Let's make a PROMISE to ourselves!

It's important to make a commitment to yourself to go through this entire process, even if it takes a year or more and not just 30 days.

Write this down, say it out loud, make a pact with a friend:
   "I am fully committed to living a life full of travel and adventure!"

This challenge can get tedious and overwhelming halfway through (there are tons of actions), but we promise you that you will come out the other side with a deeper knowledge of yourself and a toolkit of actionable travel knowledge.

The most important part of this commitment is to just try to do your best, and be easy and gentle with yourself! If you miss a day or two, or even an entire week or more, DO NOT BEAT YOURSELF UP. It is more than enough that you are making this effort and sometimes life just gets in the way.

Don't start tomorrow. Don't start next week. **START NOW!** It's like when Kaila quit smoking cigarettes; she kept waiting for the perfect time to quit. She didn't want to quit around New Year's because she knew she would be out partying and would want a social cigarette. Then, she got assigned a stressful project at work and didn't want to be extra stressed out and aggravated without having cigarettes as a crutch. Then again, she wanted to lose 10 lbs and was worried that quitting cigarettes would hurt her diet.

The list of excuses was endless. Finally, she woke up one day and decided that she was ready to start. After she fully committed to quitting, she was able to deal with each obstacle that popped up along the way.

There is no better time to start than now.

Are you excited? We know we are! We've added a little PROMISE contract below; print it out or sign it electronically. You're making a commitment to yourself to complete this challenge. Once you have signed your PROMISE contract, shoot a quick picture of it, and Tweet, Instagram, Snapchat, or YouTube it with the hashtag **#30DaysToTravel**.

By the way, we've included tons of fun printables in this challenge. You can print them out and store them in a binder along with your journal for this challenge.

Here's a link to all the downloadable printables.

You ready? Let's go!!

30-DAY TRAVEL CHALLENGE

PROMISE CONTRACT

I, _____, hereby take an oath to work with every blood, sweat, and tear that my body can muster up to complete the 30-Day Travel Challenge.

In doing so, I will:

- always have a positive mindset
- work at it each and every day, even if it's just a little
- never beat myself up for not completing tasks
- stick to it, even if I feel like giving up
- complete the challenge to help become a better version of myself

In addition to the foregoing, I promise to apply the knowledge I've gained in the 30-Day Challenge to help plan and book the best travel experience of a lifetime.

Signed by: _____

Printed Name: _____

Date: _____

2

Day 2: Journaling

Today's challenge: Try out journaling

Whew! First day over! Now we're on to Day 2, here's where all the action happens.

Now that you have signed your PROMISE agreement, we hope that you are feeling super excited about the journey ahead.

During this travel challenge, it's important to develop as much self-awareness as possible. It was shocking for us to discover how little we knew ourselves when we first took a stab at self-exploration. Many of us have never been taught the importance of self-analysis, and even if we had the desire to get a better understanding, there's no clear roadmap on how to do it correctly. As a result, many of us think that we know ourselves quite well, but there is a vast depth as to who we are just waiting to be uncovered.

Writing in a journal can help untangle all the racing thoughts in your head and calm the constant tide of emotions that seem to control and dictate your actions. This clarity of a daily writing practice helps improve your self-awareness. Writing also helps you problem-solve objectively. When you write down your problems and re-read them, you can view the situation with a new perspective. You can also revisit them in the future and learn from your past mistakes.

Journaling is really going to help on Day 4 when we start really working through our limiting beliefs about travel.

We would encourage you to journal by hand, if possible. Writing by hand allows you to feel more connected to the words you are formulating. There's a certain connection you get with your ideas when you hand write them; it's truly a fascinating difference. However, if you prefer a computer, we won't stop you. Any amount of journaling is a positive thing.

Many coaches, teachers, professionals, and entrepreneurs recommend keeping a daily journal. It may seem like a lot of writing if you're not used to sharing via paper, but don't fear! Even if you can write at least one paragraph a day, you're already ahead of the curve.

Why three pages?

Three pages is the ideal amount for a "brain-dump" or what many call "morning pages." Don't expect to win any epic writing awards from these journal entries; they are meant to take all that crap from inside your head and dump them on to paper so that you can have a clearer mind moving forward—an easier life without brain-clutter.

Three pages is also long enough for you to get past the obvious thoughts churning aimlessly in your brain. It will allow you to unveil some of the more unseen, subconscious thoughts (you'll see what I'm getting at on Day 4). We usually wake up with quite a loud chorus of jabber in our heads in the mornings (almost always negative), and these "morning pages" really help to quiet the noise pollution. It's pretty much cranking that volume knob down from a 10 to a 3.

You might be thinking, "Oh no! I've never journaled before. What should I write about? Where should I start? This seems overwhelming!" Don't think about it or plan for anything, just get started! Grab a notepad, even if it's that old, nasty one that's been sitting in your cabinet for years, and put that pen to paper. Write whatever comes to mind, whatever you are feeling, what you had for breakfast; just write! Write about the destinations that you want to travel to and the places that you've already seen.

There is no wrong way to journal. Through the process of writing, you might get stuck and run out of things to write. If this happens, just write about the fact that you're having trouble writing. Just *write*!

It's helpful to write first thing in the morning. In the mornings, it's easy to examine the dreams that you just had and your feelings during the dream.

Next, examine how you are feeling at that very moment, just to bring yourself back to the real world.

Finally, explore any issues that you are currently facing, any hopes for the day, and anything that you are excited about (usually an upcoming travel destination). After you've written that down, you'll find that three pages of content are quite easy to fill.

If you can journal successfully on a drab, regular morning, think about when you're traveling to your dream destination. Journaling on travel is the ULTIMATE best. When we're soaking in all of the new sights, sounds, and new experiences, three pages flows out of us every morning, easily and effortlessly.

What does journaling have to do with traveling? Travel is an exploration of self-discovery. The moment you start planning your travel, even all the way up to the drive home from the airport, it's truly a spiritual experience. The process of journaling allows you to record every moment of the way. Journaling should begin before you step out the door.

Diary tips:

1. **Add a date:** Adding a date to your journal can help keep things organized. When we get lost in thought, it's difficult to keep memories, tasks, feelings, and thoughts easily compartmentalized. Creating dates gives these memories a tangible way to understand and relate to your memories, especially when you look back on your entries. Plus, it's good to have them organized for future reference. Who knows, one day you might even accomplish enough to be able to write an autobiography!

2. **Draw:** Getting a little artsy is always a great way to allow the right side of your brain to take over. Drawing allows you to open up new avenues of creativity, even if you're not really the artistic type. Even adding visual aids like circles, highlights, and stars to things in your journal can help you visualize your concepts much easier. You might even find that drawing in your journal opens up even more channels of creativity that can improve your writing flow. Feel free to journal and doodle all over your writing page.

3. **Write without rules:** There is no right or wrong way of writing in a diary. Most of our diaries consist of writing that is free flowing; a jumble of whatever words spill out of our minds. We do this by scribbling non-stop.

Tim Ferriss has achieved this effortless grace in his journals. However, his style is much different. His thoughts are much more organized and thought out, which doesn't necessarily mean that's the only way to journal; it's simply another style that works for him. Ultimately, find a flow that works for you. If you like to write more meticulously, then do it! If you're more into writing anything that comes to mind, let it out on paper!

Rules inhibit creativity, and creativity is crucial for planning travel successfully. Don't let the rules of writing get in the way of your dreams.

1. **Don't evaluate your writing:** This is a creative process, and there's nothing that will hinder this exercise more than analysis and criticism of your work. Remember, no one is ever going to read these pages, so don't give a second thought to the quality. **This step is really important!**

2. **Choose a beautiful writing vessel:** If you are going to

continue this process more permanently, you're going to want a journal that motivates you to write in it. When you have a gorgeous journal to write in, it gives you a little extra magic and a creativity boost. Plus, you don't want to see your expensive journal go to waste with empty pages!

3. Again, remember that you don't have to write three pages of brilliant prose. Just **write something, anything!** Also, you don't NEED to journal every day for this challenge. It'll work even if you just write a paragraph or two daily, or even scribble a couple of sentences per day. However long you decide to write, make sure to be honest in your writing. Be an open book (hey!) when it comes to journaling. Don't be afraid to address your feelings and things you usually keep to yourself. This is for YOU and YOU alone. It will only improve the quality of your life if you are true to yourself.

We also recommend the book *The Artist's Way*; the book that first introduced us to the art of daily journaling. We started writing three pages a day in our journals after reading it. Just a month or two later, we were suddenly pursuing travel writing careers, which led to the development of this book. We never, ever thought we'd be writing a book in our careers, and this all came true because of journaling.

30-DAY TRAVEL CHALLENGE

DIARY PAGES

DATE/TIME

FEELING

3

Day 3: Meditation

Today's challenge: Start meditating for 5 minutes a day

You've made it to Day 3! Take some time to pat yourself on the back. No, seriously, actually pat yourself on your back with your hand. You've done well! Most people quit within the first 3 days of trying something new, so you're doing brilliantly.

How are you feeling about the challenge so far? Are you excited about the results you're seeing from the travel challenge?

Feeling emotionally invested and invigorated with your travel goals is all a part of the process. Even while writing this book, we find ourselves dreaming about our next goal travel destination: Okinawa, Japan. We're already visualizing ourselves enjoying fresh uni at an oceanside restaurant, and soaking in the rich culture, beautiful lands, incredible people, and unforgettable cuisine.

Now it's your turn to get just as stoked for your next travel destination.

There are quite a few new behaviors and actions heading your way, so if you don't feel excited but, instead, feel stressed or uncomfortable, that's totally ok, too! New challenges can be intimidating, but it's all about the learning process. Just take a deep breath (inhale ... exhale ... ahh, that's better) and keep on reading.

Today, we're going to challenge you to add **daily meditation** to your everyday routine. In this travel challenge, we are taking actionable steps to bring more travel into our lives; meditation will act as a bridge for your mind to reach the goals you set.

Meditation is the practice of quieting one's mind. It's easy to get caught up in the labyrinth of our minds, especially when situations are stressful or if we're at a low part in our lives. Meditating regularly assists with clearer thinking and allows us to not be at the mercy of our emotions. Essentially, meditation is the practice of being present, of being in our bodies instead of being a prisoner of our minds.

While you learn to meditate, you will find that your mind and thinking will expand. Your thoughts will be less linear and your emotions will cloud your decisions less. If you believe that you can't travel because you can't afford it, you can practice meditating on why you CAN afford to travel. Change the atmosphere in your mind and you'll change your life.

Adapting a meditation routine may initially seem intimidating, especially if you are not used to meditating at all. However, don't be alarmed. A proper meditation routine can be as simple as taking 5 minutes to yourself in silence before you get into the hustle and bustle of your day.

First, find a quiet spot where you will be undisturbed. Close your eyes, and just pay close attention to your breathing. If any thoughts come into your mind, gently push them away and again focus on your breathing. It's best to set a timer on your phone to notify you when your meditation is complete. You can also focus on the mantra, "I want to travel more" during the meditation.

Meditation has truly changed our lives. At a very prosperous period in her life, Kaila was mediating 20 minutes in the morning and another 20 minutes in the evening. Several months later, we were paid to travel all over the Midwest on tour in a rock band, performed in Macau and Malaysia working for the Hard Rock Hotels, and also booked a music tour in Japan for the next year. Working with the Hard Rock brand had always been a huge dream of ours in our music career, and we credit a big part of that manifestation to Kaila's meditation practice.

One of the most effective meditation recordings to use is "Meditations for Manifesting" by Wayne Dyer (also an author of several successful, inspirational stories). If you're not much of a reader, there are countless free and paid meditation apps to choose from.

The *Altered States* phone app is also an excellent source for guided meditation—it allows you to choose from a selection of relaxing sounds (water and soothing vibrations, as examples). You can custom-tailor your meditation by adjusting time, sounds, and other settings that will make it especially effective for you.

Another excellent phone app is *Headspace*, which is another form of guided meditation.

If you're more of the solo executer type, you don't have to use apps or tapes to practice your meditation. All you need is yourself, the right mindset, and some free, uninterrupted time. Ultimately, you need to have the time and place where you can sit comfortably for 10 minutes, or more, without any distractions.

Bonus Points: you can set up a cozy meditation corner made just for your morning meditation practice. This will make it more of a treat to get into your meditation routine every day. A comfy cushion or chair with a delicious scented candle and a warm blanket can truly be an inviting place for meditation.

It's understandable that you may accidentally miss your meditation time in a busy life; maybe your alarm went off a tad too late, or you pushed the snooze button one too many times. Have no fear! There are still many opportunities throughout the day to squeeze a meditation quickie in! Here are some examples:

1. **Stoplight senses:** Every time you hit a red stop light, you can take the opportunity to stop and clear your mind and observe your 5 senses at that moment. What do you hear, smell, taste, feel, and see? Make a conscious note of each one.

2. **Drive in silence:** In the past, we've made it a practice of ours to drive in silence and to try and stay as present as possible during the drive. During this conscious driving, make an active effort to not lose your train of thought. Observe the

license plate in front of you, hear the sounds of the cars passing, and listen to the traffic soundsc. After we did this for about 6 months, it helped us become much more centered.

3. **Play with your pet:** When you throw a ball with your dog, your mind is generally in the moment. Playing with the little feather attached to the invisible string with your cat is also a fun, interactive way to keep your mind active. Having a healthy and interactive fun time with your pets is a great way to get yourself out of your head.

4. **Exercise:** There's nothing better than getting the blood flowing and your heart pumping. Yoga is one of the best forms of meditative exercise, but an incredibly active and cardio-based workout can help get you in the right zone. It's hard to think about the stressful project at work that's due when your thighs are on fire from your 20th squat or when you're breathing hard from the 5th mile you just ran.

5. **Washing the dishes:** Some may think this is another chore to add to the list. However, it can be an excellent way to get your meditation in. If you turn the water just hot enough where you can feel it, it brings your mind back to the simple process and flow of washing. The smell of the fresh dishwashing soap and warmth from the vapors can actually be calm and soothing.

6. **Gardening:** Well, any hobby that requires the use of your hands can fall into this category. When we concentrate on making something with our hands, our focus is on something tangible, something physically real. It's important to bring your mind back to the real world, rather than be lost in thought.

7. **Have Sex:** That's right! A little consensual bumping and

grinding never really hurt anyone, but you must be present! No fantasizing about someone else with your eyes closed. Be fully present and experience every part of your partner. Pleasuring yourself works, too. Just sayin'! :P

Recommended reading: *The Power of Now*

4

Day 4: Work through your limiting travel beliefs

Today's challenge: Uncover your subconscious beliefs

Now that we have spent a little time trying out some foundational and introspective practices, it's time to analyze our thoughts.

For those of you who are a little less in-tune with your own feelings, introspection may seem like a bit much. However, you're doing a great job! Just take it one step at a time, one day at a time. You'll find that opening yourself up to ... well ... yourself, will allow you to target exactly what's holding you back mentally from traveling to your dream destinations. So now, we're finally going to start working on travel actions from this point on!

Today's assignment is to examine some of our underlying beliefs about travel that might be holding us back from our wildest travel dreams!

Life is too short to not live it to the fullest. However, our built-in belief systems can often hold us back from living out our dreams in real life. These beliefs are hard-wired and created from all the collective experiences and memories from our childhood leading all the way up to our current years, driven and cemented by pain and pleasure. These beliefs have seeped into our subconscious minds and drive our everyday behavior. If you absolutely love to travel and aren't traveling as often as you like, you probably have one or more limiting beliefs that are holding you back, whether you know it or not.

Here are some common limiting travel beliefs:
- I can't afford to travel
- I don't have time to travel
- I don't have anyone to travel with
- It's not safe to travel
- I can't get around in a foreign country when I don't speak the language
- I might get sick or lost while I'm traveling

How do we get rid of these limiting travel beliefs?

Using affirmations is pinnacle when it comes to overcoming our limiting travel beliefs. After all, the only thing that's limiting about those beliefs are the beliefs themselves. Though it may sort of seem magical and like "pie in the sky," it's anything but a quick fix. However, if you're willing to commit to working diligently at your affirmations daily, you will notice a change in your thinking, whether it's small or significant.

Your subconscious beliefs have been formed after years of repetitive thinking. For example, that one time when Mom told you, "Don't touch the hot stove!" Well, the one time you did go for the heat, it burned you. That's why your brain sends an alarming message to stay FAR away whenever you're around fire and heat.

These types of thoughts are ingrained in our thinking to PROTECT us. Makes sense, right? However, sometimes they're not always the best for us. Sometimes, we develop fears from ideas that really aren't dangerous at all; they're just unknown. Most people who haven't traveled much feel a sense of fear since it is not familiar to their everyday lives. That's why they've incorporated negative thoughts about traveling; to protect themselves from being in harm's way.

Since these negative thoughts and inhibitions have probably been instilled in our brains for a long time, they are not going to be miraculously changed and eradicated in a week. However, it's possible to feel a significant improvement in your overall thoughts, mindset, and well-being, even in just one day of practicing your affirmations.

So, what exactly are "affirmations"? Here's how to do your affirmation work ... Start by writing your affirmations down on to paper.

First, find a place that is quiet, one where you can concentrate and where you won't be disturbed, and then get to writing your affirmations.

The following are some tips on how to write ideal affirmations:
1. Start your affirmations with "I" or "my". This makes the

affirmation more direct and relatable.

2. Keep your affirmations fairly short so that you can remember them easily.

3. Write your affirmations in the present tense. You want to train your subconscious to believe these thoughts now, not somewhere in the future

4. "I am" is a great way to start an affirmation. "I want" or "I need" exemplify verbs that are for the future, not the present. Also, they aren't expressing the spirit of gratitude, which is a powerful element to incorporate into your affirmations.

5. Keep your affirmations positive. For example, instead of "I no longer fear flying," try "I love the adventure of flying and traveling the world!" Even though you may feel like you're being positive in the first statement, you don't want to let any negative words like "no" or "can't" into your thought process.

6. The more emotion and feeling that you can infuse into your affirmations, the better. For example, "I am *so excited* that I am now traveling the world!"

Here are some sample affirmations to counteract the limiting beliefs above.

I can't afford to travel.

Affirmation: My financial planning is excellent, and I have more than enough money to travel.

I don't have time to travel.

Affirmation: I have so much extra time to travel.

I don't have anyone to travel with.

Affirmation: I have great friends (or a partner) that I love to travel the world with.

It's not safe to travel.

Affirmation: I am confident and safe in all my travels.

I can't get around in a foreign country when I don't speak the language.

Affirmation: I love meeting friendly locals and traveling in exotic countries.

I might get sick or lost while I'm traveling.

Affirmation: I love to go with the flow while traveling. It always makes for a great story and experience.

How to use affirmations

So now that you've decided what your affirmations are, it's time to put them into your daily practice. The best times to do your affirmations practice are in the morning and at night time, so they're fresh in your memory when you start and end the day.

Every morning, spend at least a minute or two speaking the affirmation(s) to yourself out loud with as much feeling and gusto you can muster. Don't be afraid to get loud and in your face with it. Also, it helps to recite these in front of the mirror while maintaining eye contact with yourself (seems a little awkward, we know, but it really does help!)

The longer the time you spend on this daily exercise, the faster you will see results. If you can practice your affirmations for 5, maybe 10 minutes or more, you'll be an affirmations superstar, and have the beaming confidence to prove it.

If you want to start slow or have a roommate that hates loud noises, you can also write down your affirmations on paper over and over again (picture Bart Simpson writing on the chalkboard in the Simpsons intro).

Make sure to breathe when you are speaking your affirmations. Say them slowly with an assertive tone, ensuring that your intonations go downward. You don't want your affirmations to sound like questions or that you're unsure. If you impose any doubt, you'll feel the doubt allowing your inhibitive travel thoughts to come creeping back in. **Own them. These are YOUR affirmations. Don't let them own you!**

Remember, this isn't a quick fix and the affirmations should be a regular part of your life's routine. There's a never-ending set of beliefs that we want to improve in ourselves, so once we are finished with one affirmation, we just get to work on the next one. We're little, self-help energizer bunnies, and we're kind of addicted to it!

5

Day 5: Decide where you want to go next

Today's challenge: Find your next dream destination!

Finally, we're getting to the fun stuff! Today, you get to decide where you want to travel next. That's right! We're finally starting to see the light at the end of the tunnel, and boy does it look good!

Earlier this year, both Kaila's mastermind group and her coach pushed her to make a list of the places that she wanted to travel to this year. She was a bit frustrated with this task and found it to be unnecessary because she simply want to travel everywhere in the world that she haven't been yet. She certainly wasn't going to make a list of everywhere she hadn't been—the list would be way too long!

Luckily, they continued to push her to write down a list of 12 locations, traveling once a month to a new location, and she finally put the pen to the paper. A month and a half later, we were both on a plane to India (near the top of her list of destinations) and had two offers for other destinations on the list. That is the power of getting specific with your goals, which is exactly what we're going to cover today.

Have an idea already of where you want to head to next? Maybe you've been dreaming of that luxury getaway to Bali with your girlfriends. Perhaps you finally want to take that motorcycle tour across the Gobi desert for 2 weeks. Wherever the road may take you, spend some time today familiarizing yourself with your dream destination. Scour the internet for all the info about excursions, sites, history, culture, landmarks, shopping, and food; all the goods! Start getting EXCITED about your dream vacation.

When we plan our dream travel destinations, the first thing we check is if Anthony Bourdain has filmed a past episode in that location. Not only is he truly one of our heroes, but he's also a legend at finding the best places to eat across the globe.

We are both HUGE foodies, so good food is definitely a mandatory priority when it comes to travel for us. It's also helpful to read books that are either about your dream destination, written by someone from your dream destination, or takes place in your dream destination. You can also do the same with movies if you're not a big reader, which is probably not the case since you are reading this book, after all.

If you haven't zeroed in on your next travel destination yet, here are some brainstorming ideas:

Ask yourself why

Here are some things to consider when selecting your destination:

1. How long you want to travel for
2. A rough idea of your budget
3. Are you aiming for international or domestic travel?
4. Do you want to make all your travel decisions, do you want to join a tour, or go to an all-inclusive resort?
5. Is your travel event-related? Dreaming of going to Coachella or The Olympics?
6. Do you want a special experience when you travel? A yoga retreat or running with the bulls?

Choose your environment

Are you the type that wants to spend long days on the beach in a sun-soaked tropical paradise, or snowboard down snow-capped mountains in a far off locale? Maybe you prefer to fully immerse yourself into a foreign culture with a burning desire to learn the language and customs before you leave. Or, perhaps you are the type that wants to stick to a place where you can get around easily with English.

These are all key points to keep in mind when you pick the environment for your vacation.

Remember, it's not just a place you're traveling to. It's what you'll be doing and who you'll be interacting with that determines your environment.

Explore "best of" lists

One of the best ways to look up excellent places to visit is to literally look up the best places to visit. Why do all the grunt work when someone has already done it for you? There are many compilations of "best of" lists that will help you decide where to travel to.

These can include anything ranging from "the best beach resorts," "the best budget-friendly destinations," "the best luxury travel experience," etc. Some popular lists include the New York Times' 52 Places to Go in 2019 or Lonely Planet's Best in Travel 2019

Travel magazines

Although we currently live in a digital world, there's something extremely satisfying about the smell and feel of a hard copy magazine. Take an hour out of your schedule and sift lazily and leisurely through travel magazines. Most travel magazines feature a multitude of destinations per issue, so you get the best bang for your buck and a little extra inspiration. Excellent magazines for inspiration are *National Geographic Travel*, *Travel and Leisure*, and *Afar and Saveur*."

One of the best ways to get travel information straight to your screen is to subscribe to several travel magazines on the *Texture* iPhone app (for one single monthly, affordable subscription fee).

If you're trying to save money, you can just go to your local library for many of these magazines or back issues. You can even hit up your local grocery store and read creepily in the aisles, although we wouldn't really suggest it unless you're REALLY budgeting for that dream trip to Peru.

Tripzard

Tripzard is a fun and interactive way to get your travel plans and inspiration in check. All you have to do is answer a quick survey about the things that you are looking for in an ideal vacation. Tripzard does the work for you and will give you roughly 10 suggestions.

We are pretty big fans of lazy and tropical destinations. After we answered all the questions about our desired trip, Tripzard gave us a couple of suggestions that we would have never considered on our own, such as Madagascar, Tangiers, Morocco, Mozambique, Tanzania, and many more!

Here are a couple other sites that are similar to Tripzard:
http://besttripchoices.com/
http://www.jauntaroo.com/

Hotel or Airbnb

If you are planning on spending most of your time relaxing by the pool or at your own private beach/villa, you might want to start your travel planning by choosing your dream hotel or Airbnb, instead. This step is crucial, especially if you are looking for an all-inclusive hotel where everything is provided for you. Sometimes, designer hotels can spark inspiration for an entire trip. Plus, most hotel websites will have a plethora of information about the area, so you can essentially plan your entire trip around the hotel excursions, location, and accommodation.

Subscribe to flight deals websites

For one of our trips last year, we chose the destination because we saw an exciting deal on one of the flight deal websites that we subscribe to. The website was *Travel Pirates*, and they were offering a great deal on a tour and flight deal package: A 10-day trip from the south to the north of Vietnam. Kaila had the app downloaded to her phone and checked it daily to see the latest travel deals—it was really simple!

Another trick is to follow their Travel Pirates Facebook page and set their notifications to feature "all posts" on your feed. This way, you can get all the updates directly at the top of your feed so you don't miss any deals. Since you probably follow many Facebook pages already, setting this feature makes sure that you can see their daily deals on the top of your Facebook feed.

Here are some other great websites to follow:
- The Flight Deal
- Next Vacay
- Expedia
- Viator
- Travelzoo
- TripAdvisor
- Kayak

Join a forum

Sometimes you can get the best advice directly from other people. However, you can't exactly have coffee with someone in Namibia when you're planning your trip. Fortunately, forums are here to save the day!

Head into your favorite Facebook travel group, or a thread on Reddit or Quora, and ask for recommendations from other travelers. Or, you can just ask the question on your personal Facebook page and other travel-related Facebook groups. If you just ask, "Where do you recommend for my next vacation destination?" you'll find a lot of people are pretty stoked to talk about their most recent trips.

6

Day 6: Be a local tourist

Today's challenge: Explore your city

How are you feeling? You're already almost done with your first week. It's crazy how fast time flies! Before you know it, you'll be at the end of this 30-day journey, and in a blink of an eye, you'll be looking back while sipping a piña colada on the beach, or climbing the peaks of Mt. Everest, or whatever your dream trip may be!

For now, we're going to start pumping those travel muscles by segueing on a little side adventure to a local travel destination. If you absolutely cannot go today, don't fret. You don't NEED to go today but try to set up your local trip in the next week or so. But hey, it's a great excuse to get out of the house, so try and make it happen.

Even though you may think you know your city inside out, there are tons of ways to explore your hometown for a mini staycation. Most people get so distracted about how the grass is greener away from home they forget to cherish the beauty and delight of what's directly in their backyard. Even if you live out in the sticks or somewhere where there's not a lot happening, don't worry. You can even explore your neighboring city or get really creative and do something fun in nature.

So, it's time to act like a tourist in your own city. You might already know the hot spots in your city and the sights that you haven't made time to see yet. If so, you can skip this next section and be on your way. Either way, even if you have a local excursion in mind, it's fun to try some of the tactics below to discover exciting excursions in your town.

Here are some ideas on how to find fun things to do locally:

Purchase a guidebook about your city or search online for "(Your City) travel guides." Plenty of options should pop and you may even find tailored guides. For example: "A Culture Lover's Guide to Houston," or "A Food Guide to Las Vegas."

Visit a local hotel and scope out the shelves with tri-fold pamphlets of things to do. This is a great way to discover the local tourism industry and even make some friendly connections. You can even speak to the person at the front desk for advice on recommended things to do in town. Once you have a place in mind, remember that you can call to see if there are local discounts. The public library is also a good resource for new local events and cultural announcements.

Sites like TripAdvisor have a solid listing of excursions and things to do. There are a ton of activities and tours that you can purchase but also plenty of details and ample information about free activities.

Visit your local tourism board website for your city or state. The tourism board spends tons of cash on promoting your city to tourists, and are always trying to boost tourism in your city. They will likely have the most updated information about fun things to do in your area.

If you don't feel like doing the extra in-depth research, perhaps something from the list below will give you an idea.

Excursions that you can do now:

Take a "jump on jump off" bus tour: These bus tours are usually pretty cheap, and give you a completely different perspective of your home city. If you live in a smaller town, you might need to go to a nearby, bigger city to experience one of these fun tours. If you're not really a fan of long drives on a bus, there are usually tours on bikes or even Segway tours, depending on what your city offers. The key is to get out and explore your city from a different viewpoint!

Be an Instagram tourist: Find those cheesy tourist spots in your city and take photos in front of them. Kaila, surprisingly, lives five minutes away from the Hollywood Walk of Fame (you know, where the sidewalks are covered with stars and famous actors' names). One day, she decided to walk it with a friend and she found it was shockingly delightful! Also, they even discovered a cute restaurant they would have never been to if they didn't explore by foot.

You can even make a list of the best places to take photos in your city and aim to take a photo there. If you're alone, snap a selfie! It makes a fun photo collage and an interesting journey trying to find the perfect photo spots you probably wouldn't have gone to on a regular day.

Eat at the local tourist trap: Pink's Hot Dogs is one of the most iconic tourist destinations in Hollywood, and Kaila lives in walking distance from it! She drives past it practically every day and marvels at how there is always a line at their hot dog stand, morning and night, rain or shine. As a disinterested Angeleno, she would also make fun of these noobs who would wait in line for hours for a mere hot dog. One day, when driving by, she saw that the line was much shorter than usual, and so jumped in line. The menu was nothing like she imagined, and she enjoyed one of the most delicious hot dogs that she'd ever had! There truly is a reason that Pink's is a tourist trap, and she was just always too jaded to see it. Find your local restaurant hot spot and give it a go—you never know how delicious and fantastic it might actually be, especially if so many people are taking the time to wait for the food.

Explore your local outdoors: California is famous for its beaches, but did you know that most Californians never even visit the beach? It's shocking how much people don't explore their own area. That's why it's time to discover the hidden gems right outside your front door. Is your town famous for its fishing, mountains, hiking, or skiing? Try out an outdoor excursion like kayaking, or explore a new hike in nature that you never knew about. You can also check TrailLink for local hiking, walking, and biking trails in your area.

Have a friend be your tour guide: You know that one friend who can't stop talking about what's happening in your city? Ask them to be your personal tour guide. Plus, it'll be a great opportunity to catch up and bond. You'll be surprised by what other people might find interesting, and it's really fun to see your city through someone else's eyes. You can always treat them to lunch or dinner as an extra incentive (who doesn't love free food?)

Rent a hotel or Airbnb for the night: If you have a little extra spending money, stay the night outside of your place in your city. Planning a staycation in your home town is the best way to get your travel juices flowing, and an awesome way to practice your planning skills on a smaller scale. Plus, you get the same satisfaction for travel without having to go far or call off work.

Download a city guide from the app store: There are endless free and paid city guides on your phone's app store. They even offer narrated city guides options; it's really like having a personal tour guide with you the whole way (in your pocket!) Here is a narrated city guide with tours in over 100 cities: VoiceMap Audio Tours

7

Day 7: Rest

Congratulations! You've officially made it through the first week. It wasn't that bad, right? Feel free to share your experience by emailing us or contacting us through our social media channels. We'd love to receive feedback about your journey.

30-day challenges can definitely be quite overwhelming, but they are a great way to make a short, digestible commitment to making a positive change in your life. It's called a challenge for a reason! Adding a 30-day challenge can be a big addition to our already hectic and fast-paced lives. Sometimes, we even find that our lives get even more stressful when we commit to the new schedule. Suddenly, we're faced with surprise trips, new job offers, new relationships, etc. When you put more effort into making yourself a better version of you, you'll find that more opportunities will follow.

The first 30-day challenge that we completed was a life-changer! We admit, we attempted several of these types of challenges and only made it 50-75% of the way through. Somewhere along the way, life would make an appearance and our interest would slowly drift off.

The challenge that we ended up finally completing involved changing our perspectives of money. It required an hour a day taking four actions surrounding money, in the categories of earning, finding new leads, self-care, and spirituality. We teamed up with three of our friends to do the challenge, and we strongly believe that teaming up with others helped us to finish the 30-day journey, through and through.

Pursuing the money challenge really impacted our lives in a good way. We had decided to pursue music full-time and quit another thriving but time-consuming career to pursue our music dreams. We had been struggling for more than a year and were just getting by working difficult promo jobs, which left us feeling disheartened and unmotivated. We were desperate for a change.

At first, it was rather easy to implement the steps of the money challenge into our everyday lives. However, the tides quickly turned. Suddenly, halfway through, Kaila booked an unconventional part-time job working graveyard hours, making it really difficult to stick to our daily commitments. However, her saving grace was the support group and friends. Without them, she would have let the negative thoughts and stress get the best of her and would never have finished the challenge.

As a result of taking on the money challenge, she interviewed for a job and scored it! It was the ideal part-time job; it paid well and allowed her to pursue her passion for music, full-time. It was such a perfect fit that she ended up working with the company for three years, working from home and making money in her pajamas! The challenge itself allowed her to open doors to opportunities she would have NEVER pursued.

Please, if you feel disheartened any time during the challenge, come back and reread the above story. We were both at an all-time low in our lives, with no direction and little money. But, because we stuck to the challenge, changed our mindset, and found a strong support group, we were able to turn our lives around. It is totally possible and you CAN do it!

For today, it's time to rest and recharge. You've been working diligently hard, so it's time to take a break. If you enjoyed the journaling and the meditation days, feel free to continue the meditating and journaling today, or take the day off from the challenge completely. It's totally up to you.

If you like, you could spend today reflecting on anything that you've learned from this week's challenges. What were your biggest wins this week? Where would you like to see improvement? Reflect on your current feelings—are you happy, sad, or anxious? Don't worry if you aren't feeling happy yet; this challenge can stir up a lot of emotions along the way, and you could feel a full range of emotions throughout the experience. Allow those feelings to flow in and out of you.

If you have a friend doing the challenge with you, now is a good time to do a quick phone call. Limit it to 15 minutes and share the insights that you have both learned along the way. Otherwise, give yourself a pat on the back. Week 1, DONE!

30-DAY TRAVEL CHALLENGE

WEEK 1 REFLECTION

WHAT WERE THE BIGGEST CHALLENGES THIS WEEK?

_____

_____

_____

HOW MANY TIMES DID YOU COMPLETE

JOURNALING: _____

MEDITATION: _____

AFFIRMATIONS: _____

WHICH LOCATION DID YOU CHOOSE AND WHY?

_____

_____

DESCRIBE YOUR LOCAL DAY TRIP.

_____

_____

_____

_____

_____

30-DAY TRAVEL CHALLENGE

WEEK 1 REFLECTION

WHAT WAS YOUR FAVORITE PART OF WEEK 1?

_____
_____
_____

WHAT WOULD YOU LIKE TO IMPROVE ON?

_____
_____
_____
_____
_____
_____
_____
_____
_____
_____
_____
_____

II

Week 2: Finding Inspiration

8

Day 8: Reading

Ohhhhh yeah! You've made it to Week 2. Week 1 wasn't so bad, was it?

In Week 1, we focused more on self-reflection and getting to know ourselves and our feelings better. You did a lot of writing and probably paid more attention to your internal self than ever before. It's vital to build a foundation before charging forward into the complexities of travel planning. You would hate for all of your hard work to collapse because you don't have a strong base.

This week, we're going to amp it up a bit. It's time that mama bird pushes her chicklets out of the nest. Don't worry, you WILL fly!

While the first week may have dug up some more difficult feelings, some of these daily tasks in Week 2 may give you a little caffeine-like charge, a little bit of a natural high. This next upcoming challenge won't take any extra time out of your day, and you can incorporate it seamlessly into your life (unless you work at home, then make an effort to go out for a quick coffee run, at least!)

So let's get started!

Today's challenge: Read a book that inspires you to travel

Before we start: If you've been keeping up daily, you should already notice an improvement in your mindset. In just one week of practicing meditation, affirmations, and maintaining a positive mindset, you are already closer to the confident and strong mentality that's required to making your travel dreams come to life. Of course, it's not an instant, magical cure; however, each small action compounds. You're slowly building a foundation for your outlook on life that can last you eternally.

Before we get started with this task, just remember that you should keep using the past daily actions that made you feel good and that resonated with you.

Now, let's get kicking on Day 8!

Have you ever been so engrossed in a novel that you forget the time? You suddenly check the clock and a few hours have passed, which only felt like minutes. Stories and novels are miraculous inventions that can truly take us to other worlds, allowing our creativity to unfold and create elaborate images of adventure, romance, and action, in the comfort of our own homes. Reading is so important because it exposes you to new ideas and concepts that you might not encounter in your daily life. It is just like a form of travel without having to leave the couch.

We are going to focus on travel books for today. Your task is to find a travel book, buy it, and read at least one chapter of it. If you don't want to invest any money in purchasing another book, just below is a list we made of 9 great reads that we recommend for any soon-to-be traveler.

How-to books about travel

How to Travel the World on $50 a Day: Revised: Travel Cheaper, Longer, Smarter
See Book Here

Matt, the mastermind of the ever-popular blog Nomadic-Matt.com, came out with a popular book where he teaches readers how to travel the world on a budget. He provides step-by-step instructions and demonstrates that travel is accessible to everyone. Read this book if you still seriously believe that you can't afford to travel.

Vagabonding
See Book Here

For those of you considering long-term travel or dream of nomadic life, this is a great book to teach you how to live life as a permanent traveler. Vagabonding is defined by author Rolf Potts as taking an extended vacation from life to live your life as you please. He gives you all the nitty-gritty details about living your life in constant travel mode and how to budget for this kind of lifestyle.

The 4-Hour Workweek
See Book Here

Tim Ferriss is the ultimate guru for our lives. He is total **#goals** for me! *The 4-Hour Workweek* is my personal bible.

Kaila once started a book club with one of her closest friends, and this was the book that they read first. A couple years after studying the book, both of us have created 'muses' (aka passive income machines), and we are now traveling once a month internationally on media trips (where we don't have to pay for the expenses). In this book, Ferriss teaches his principles about how to design your ideal work-balanced life. Ferriss educates the reader on how to work less and travel more with real-world templates and case studies to back it up.

Big Travel, Small Budget: How to Travel More, Spend Less, and See the World
See Book Here

This book annihilates the idea that travel is expensive and cost prohibitive. Similar to Vagabonding, Ryan Shauers focuses his travel concepts on long-term travel. Even if you're not planning on doing any long-term travel adventures abroad, this is an excellent, inspirational read that could get your mindset in travel-ready mode.

Books that will inspire you to travel

1,000 Places to See Before You Die: Revised Second Edition
See Book Here

A New York Times bestseller, this book shares the most unforgettable places and experiences that you have to see in your lifetime, featuring full-color photos. The title is pretty self-explanatory!

The Geography of Bliss: One Grump's Search for the Happiest Places in the World
See Book Here

This unique book is about a writer's journey exploring some of the happiest places on Earth. It's a clever read that will make you laugh out loud, but it'll also make you examine what happiness means, not only to you but worldwide. Eric Weiner strives to discover why people in North Carolina are so happy, and whether people in the Netherlands or Thailand are any happier than the rest of the world. He also concludes as to where the happiest place on earth is, so it's worth reading on just to find out how he comes to that conclusion!

The Beach
See Book Here

You might have already seen the movie starring Leonardo Dicaprio, however, the book, as usual, is far better than the film. Don't be surprised if Thailand is the next travel destination on your list. It's also just a fascinating read to delve into one backpacker's search for an untouched paradise, which brings him to confront some serious life lessons and moral choices.

The Alchemist
See Book Here

This book is a modern classic about the journey for treasure far and wide, and the ultimate discovery that the treasure is within yourself. Paulo Coelho's defining story is about Santiago, an Andalusian shepherd boy with an undying need to travel the world. Throughout his journey, he learns about foundational wisdom coming from within our hearts, and seeing opportunities and learning to take them while being wary of distractions and dangers, and, ultimately, to live out his dreams.

Eat Pray Love
See Book Here

This enticing book is about a woman who has all the trappings of the American Dream but is deeply unhappy. She leaves it all behind to explore Italy, India, and Bali and finds her true self. It has inspired many women to travel more and has especially helped to spark the trend of female solo travel.

Can you commit to reading one book this month? This week? Today?

Tim Ferriss (my God) has said that he reads one book a day. He says that it's the best way to get a university-level education without setting yourself back tens of thousands of dollars. Check out his speed reading tutorial which demonstrates how he is able to read so much daily!

A great way to "read" lots to listen to books on tape. You can easily get through a book a week during your commutes and daily driving schedule. We personally subscribe to Audible, and we love it!

For those of you who don't want to purchase an additional book or audiobook, you can check out AFAR or Longreads—long articles about travel that you can access for free, online!

9

Day 9: Watch an inspirational travel movie

Today's challenge: Grab some popcorn and catch a travel flick!

Today, we're giving you a slight break from all the hard work that you have been actively putting in! All you have to do today is watch a travel movie (or a travel television show if you are crunched for time).

Why watch a travel movie? Similar to the activity of reading travel books, movies can inspire and motivate you just as much as a good book can. You can also use a movie that takes place in your dream destination as a tool to learn more about the culture and overall ambiance.

At this point, you should begin to live, breathe, and dream travel. Traveling should be your ultimate obsession from this point forward. This fervent thought will allow you to pursue your travel goals unstoppably. You will get through to the end of this challenge if you are inspired, motivated, and passionate.

Here are a few excellent travel movies. If you happen to discover any on your own, feel free to send us an email with your picks!

Eat Pray Love

Almost as good as the book, this movie is a fun and romantic way to fall in love with travel. Julia Roberts is stunningly charming, as always. Her adventures make you want to chow down on all the decadent cuisine of Italy, find the meaning to your life in India, and enjoy the bliss and beauty of Bali.

Up in the Air

Up in the Air illuminates this secret world of free travel perks and hacks, and, of course, George Clooney charms throughout. The movie also teaches that there is a difference between using travel as escapism and using travel to transform and enhance your life.

Seven Years in Tibet

This movie was adapted from the book and is based on a true story about Heinrich Harrer, played by Brad Pitt. *Seven Years in Tibet* takes us through the character of Harrer, a hardened Austrian mountain climber who eventually develops true compassion, and learns to understand a new and unfamiliar culture. As a viewer, you fully experience first-hand the kindness of the Tibetan people, who appreciate life to the fullest. During Harrer's time in Tibet with the Dalai Lama, he was truly transformed as a human being.

The Secret Life of Walter Mitty

Walter Mitty is absolutely bored at his day job and escapes the monotony of his life in his beautiful and elaborate daydreams. His job finally sends him on the ultimate adventure to find the perfect photo. He, suddenly, is faced with a remarkable adventure as he travels around the world to find it. The cinematography in this movie is so unforgettably beautiful that you'll personally want to visit all the destinations!

Lost in Translation

A washed-up movie star and a young college student make an unlikely connection in a Tokyo hotel. These two characters, although very different, are quite similar since they feel so lost in their own lives. As they are both strangers in a foreign land, they find escape, understanding, and a connection in an unfamiliar world. This movie was shot entirely in Japan (one of Kaila's favorite places in the world) and emulates the sense of culture shock that you experience (from a Western perspective) when you first visit the country.

Into The Wild

Into the Wild is based on the true story about Emory University graduate Christopher McCandless. He gives up all of his personal possessions and wanders the Alaskan wilderness. Along the way, he forges connections with unique characters who each change his life in their own way, all against the epic beauty of the Alaskan background.

If you don't have Netflix, Amazon, iTunes, or simply don't want to spend any additional money renting a movie, jump onto YouTube and check out some of these channels for free:

Strictly Dumpling

FunForLouis

Vagabrothers

Migrationology

10

Day 10: Join a community

Today's Challenge: Join at least ONE travel community

We just wanted to check in with you before we dive right into Day 10. If you're feeling a little overwhelmed with each daily task, take a deep breath and pause for a moment. Repeat this:

"I am fully capable of completing this challenge!"

You CAN do it. Don't let that evil voice in your head tell you otherwise.

Now let's begin Day 10.

Joining a travel community is a great way to connect with other travelers. Developing connections and networking is such an important step on your travel journey. Not only will you meet new friends that you could possibly travel with, but you'll also be fully immersed in the travel mindset when you're surrounded by like-minded people.

These groups will also supply you with a fresh resource of tips and tricks on traveling, from the most luxurious destinations to rough and tough areas of intrigue. You'll also be introduced to new destinations that you've never heard of that you can add to your bucket list.

Not everyone in your personal life may be as passionate and knowledgeable about travel as you would like them to be, so this is a great way to take your passion for travel to the next level.

We're listing several community resources below, and today's challenge only requires you to choose one community to join, but feel free to join as many as you like! We got a little crazy excited one night and joined every single relevant travel community Facebook group in existence. However, it's been extremely beneficial since we've found sponsored travel opportunities because of it! You never know what you'll find and where you'll find it when it comes to Facebook groups.

Facebook groups

Facebook groups are a great way to join a community without leaving your house. Passionate travelers all over the world join these groups and share their inspirations daily. There are literally thousands of Facebook groups on the topic of travel alone, but here are some notable ones:

We See The World Bloggers

If you are interested in getting into the world of travel blogging, this is a great resource. Bloggers collaborate frequently in this group and are often exchanging guest post articles to bring more visibility to their respective blogs as a team.

Girls LOVE Travel®

This is one of the largest, female-centric travel groups on Facebook, with over 300,000 members. When we joined, we were surprised to see that some of our girlfriends were already members of the group. The last time we posted a photo from our journeys it was featured on their Instagram page, with over 80,000 followers!

Nomad Island

This group is truly one of a kind. The members are discussing the necessary steps that it takes to purchase an island that would be welcoming of all cultures and languages. Members of the group have actually conducted research into the possibility of this, which you can read about it in the group. If they do end up purchasing an island, you definitely want to be a part of it, so join today!

Award Travel 101®

If you are addicted to travel hacking or want to learn all about it, this is a great community of like-minded travel hackers. Travel hacking makes it possible for anyone to travel in luxury for a fraction of the price, or even for free! (Read on to the end of the book to check out an interview from Richard Kerr, the founder of

Award Travel 101®)

Let There Be Travel

This is a general travel group that is open to anyone who loves to travel. They occasionally plan group trips for their Facebook group and are very actively engaged in giving advice and helping with tips about travel planning.

In-person travel communities

In-person meetups are a great way to network and make deeper connections than you may make behind the screen of a computer. Here are some suggestions for some of the best:

Meetup

Meetup is a great resource for networking groups in every city. Search your respective city to see if there is an active travel-based meetup group; one in which you can network with others suffering from wanderlust.

Wanderful

Wanderful is a women's travel society. Check to see if there's a chapter open in your city. If not, think about starting one! *Wanderful* is searching for city leaders all over the world. If you are deeply involved in the local travel community, you will up your traveling game tenfold because of networking, access to information, and being fully immersed in the travel world. This is an empowering and uplifting international sisterhood of female travelers. (Read on to the end of the book to check out an interview from Beth Santos, the founder of *Wanderful*)

Travel Massive

This is more of a travel industry networking group. However, if you have a blog or travel-related social media account, you will qualify as a member. *Travel Massive* has chapters all over the world and, of course, you can look into opening a chapter if one has not already started in your city. *Travel Massive* hosts some of the most resourceful meetups; often the host of the meetup is a tourism board, airline, hotel or travel-related company. They always have delicious food and drinks served from the countries that the hosting company is from—a little incentive to get your booty off the couch for a free bite to eat.

Misc. online communities

Reddit/travel/

If you know Reddit, you'll know that it's an extremely useful resource for any topic under the sun. This specific subreddit is a place to network and share your most amazing travel photos. Bear in mind that if you haven't used Reddit before, it takes some getting used to the platform. You can't join the Reddit page as easily as a Facebook group. However, you can subscribe and speak to the other community members there or just peruse the conversation for great information.

Quora International Travel

This Quora group cannot be joined, but you can follow the discussion for updates. It's mostly filled with insightful discussions about international travel. You can also feel free to post any inquiries that you have about travel.

Nomad List

Nomadlist is the only community on this list that requires a membership fee. It's designed for those who want to work remotely all around the world and crowdsources the best places to work. If you are serious about working remotely, this is a must-join community.

Blog

One of the best ways to really get integrated with the online travel world is to start a blog. It's a great way to network and create a public journal/diary of your favorite travels. We absolutely love having a travel blog; it's a great place for us to share tips and tricks with friends and followers.

Don't be intimidated! Setting up a WordPress blog yourself is not costly, and you can register a domain name for around $10. You can also set up a free Tumblr or Blogspot account, etc.

Feel free to update the blog as infrequently as once a year; that way, you won't be held back by the pressure of having to produce regular content. It's just like your own personal travel diary but posted online for anyone to see!

All in all, it's important to join these types of communities. Even if you work better alone, these types of communities can give you valuable insight and a different perspective on travel that you may not have seen.

So, join at LEAST one community today!

11

Day 11: Start a travel fund

Today's Challenge: Start putting aside money for travel

Can you believe that we are already one-third of the way through the challenge? You should be proud that you've already tackled such a sizable portion. It's happening, it's really happening, and you're doing great!

Now that you have made some vital steps toward your travel dreams, it's time to get into the thing that we're mostly concerned about on a daily basis: Money.

Today, we're going to start a travel fund. This can be as simple as setting aside a physical, dedicated money jar in the house and depositing $20 bucks a month, or as involved as going to the bank to open up a separate savings account.

Let's dive into some of your options below.

Open a travel savings account

Capital One

Capital One is the online savings account that we personally use for travel and everything else that we are saving up for. If you are serious about traveling, we highly recommend this method! Capital One is a no-fee and no-minimum savings account that's based entirely online.

Inside Capital One, we've set up multiple mini savings accounts for larger purchases that we are saving up for. We have a travel fund, a drone fund (currently obsessed with drone flying—an expensive habit), a new camera lens fund, and more. What's great is that you can set up an endless amount of mini savings accounts for all your needs.

After we set up new savings accounts on Capital One, we have them programmed to automatically debit $25, $50, $100 or more weekly, bi-monthly, or monthly from our checking accounts into the respective savings accounts. It's really a sweet surprise to find that we magically have more money than we thought. It's an extremely effective "set it and forget it" method. For example, last year we discovered that we had plenty of funds to take a 10-day tour to Vietnam with some girlfriends. Boom! No need to save or spend extra; it was already there waiting for us to spend!

The one thing that you need to know about the Capital One account is that it usually takes a couple of days for you to transfer the money back into your savings account. This could be a problem if you really need to extract emergency funds. However, we prefer this delay in transfer because it makes us really think about our purchases a little more carefully. We never end up using the money that we saved in our Capital One accounts for impulse purchases.

Regular savings account

Setting up a regular savings account is an excellent way to keep adding to a travel fund. In most cases, there is zero cost to set up a savings account if you already have a checkings account with the bank. Make sure to check with your bank about the exact requirements before going and opening any savings account.

It will also be helpful to set up an ATM account for such accounts. One of the great parts of having an ATM account connected to your travel savings account is you can keep all of your incoming and outgoing funds in one place. If you're out traveling and need to take out a bit of cash for some souvenirs at a stand, you can pull money directly out of this account, and so you can keep an accurate account for where money is leaving. This will also give you a very clear and easy way of tracking your travel expenses.

You can also set up automatic transfers from your checkings account to your savings account—similar to the Capital One savings account.

Piggy bank

Also known as a change jar, simply deposit all your change into a physical travel fund jar! This can add up quickly if you save up for a year, and it's so much fun taking the change jar to the supermarket change machine to see how much you've accumulated.

We would also encourage you to throw an extra $5, $10 or $20 into it on a regular basis to grow your travel piggy bank quicker.

12

Day 12: Attend a travel conference

Today's challenge: Find out the dates of local travel events

It's time to kick up your networking skills into the next gear.

Looking for the ultimate inspiration? Attend a travel conference. If you live in the US, there are several major travel conferences taking place throughout the year, and they are goldmines for planning your dream travel adventure.

One of our favorites is the *Travel and Adventure Show*, which keeps expanding everywhere; it takes place all over the US. You really need a couple of days to walk through some of the major conventions—there are often hundreds of vendors, tons of free trip raffles, travel seminars and workshops, free samples and food, and all kinds of stuff. Tickets to the Travel Adventure Show are only $15 for a one-day pass. If you have a blog, you can also apply for a free media pass!

If there is a travel conference in town, you should definitely make an effort to attend it. Otherwise, look up upcoming travel conventions in your vicinity and schedule it in.

Here is a list of travel shows in the United States: https://10times.com/usa/travel-tourism/tradeshows

No conference taking place near you or anytime soon? Look for smaller travel events or seminars. We searched on Eventbrite and found several travel-themed events, such as "Let's Travel like an Insider," which was a free event, and "All about Travel Photography," which was a paid, ticketed event.

Even if you can't just pack up and attend a travel conference (that may not even exist today), you should definitely solidify a conference that you WILL be able to attend before you plan your trip. Today, take the time to mark your calendar and find the right conference that works for you. If you can't go today, buy your ticket. That way, you're locked in and can't back out last minute (because that darn evil voice of negativity in your head is feeling antisocial).

Conferences are great places to network with people in the travel industry. Also, there are many representatives from hotels, tourism boards, excursions, and other travel-related companies that you can schmooze with. You never know who you'll meet and who just might like you so much they give you a sweet discount or even a free upgrade!

One of the best tactics at conferences is to collect as many business cards as possible, especially if the conference is huge.

Later, when you get back to your home, you can enter their information in a filing system (whether it's your computer, phone, or Rolodex if you're old school). Before your trip, be sure to reach out to them stating that you met them at the conference. Even if you didn't, and it's a huge company, they may just pretend to remember you and appreciate the fact that you reached out. This tactic can often lead to coupons, upgrades, and sponsorships.

When you attend the conference, be sure to be ready and personable. Never negate anyone that you meet; you never know who they are or who they know. Always be friendly and open to conversation. Bring your best social skills and kick some networking butt!

13

Day 13: Connect with a traveler

Build your travel circleToday's Challenge:

Yes! You're almost at the finish line for Week 2. Keep up the amazing work!

Get your best networking and social skills warmed because you're about to meet and connect with a fellow traveler.

Most of us know a world wanderer. You know, that one friend who travels the world and posts all of their incredible vacation photos on social media while you're at work diligently getting through paperwork. Instead of feeling envious, change your mindset and be inspired by taking out this intrepid traveler to lunch. Yup, a little reverse psychology is actually going to be your best friend today.

If you don't already have a group of friends that frequently travel, it's important to start to make an effort in getting some. We become most like the 10 people that we spend the most time with.

So, if you want to be a traveler, you need to build up your network of travelers, pronto! Go back to Day 10 and reach out to some of the active travelers that you have observed in one of the new communities, and don't be afraid to say hello! The worst thing that can happen is they won't respond and you're pretty much back to square one. Put yourself out there and take charge. You can do it!

Do your best to stifle the shyness, especially for the fellow introverts out there. Think of it as if the roles were reversed; if someone reached out to you, you'd probably want to connect! If your friend or potential mentor target is not a travel professional, they probably don't get bombarded for travel advice, so they are likely to be flattered by your request.

If you can parlay lunch into a travel mentorship, where your friend can guide you on your upcoming travel journeys, then you've hit the travel networking jackpot. Getting to meet someone in person is a whole different dynamic. You can also build stronger relationships by having an in-person discussion and learn more about your mentor (especially since they can't randomly sign offline on you).

If you already have a friend who travels a lot, just go ahead and ask! If you are reaching out to someone who you are less familiar with, here are some tips and tricks for asking an acquaintance or a stranger for mentorship:

Tips for asking an acquaintance or stranger for mentorship

Check your connections if you are reaching out to a totally cold lead

It's always easier to reach out if you have some sort of connection to that person, whether it's your sister's best friend's cousin or someone you've met briefly at a conference. If you are reaching out to a stranger or a distant acquaintance, check LinkedIn or Facebook to see if you have any mutual friends that can help make an introduction for you.

If you don't have any mutual connections, write them a personal note. Say that you've loved watching their travel journeys on Facebook or Instagram or love their recent post in the Facebook group that you are both a member of. You can also mention if you went to the same college, have the same taste in music, or if they have gone to one of your bucket list destinations. The more personal your email or message is, the more likely it is to get a response.

Be prepared and make your question specific

Don't lead with a vague question like, "Can you teach me how to travel more?" Get really specific with your questions. Before reaching out, research what exactly it is that you want to learn from that person specifically.

Did you want to learn about budget travel or how to use points and credit cards to travel for free since your potential mentor wrote a blog post on budget travel hacking? Or you might just want to get tips on traveling to the southern border of Russia, where your mentor stayed in a yurt for two weeks. Make your question specific and clear before you go into the meeting so that you don't waste their time or your own.

Cater to the meeting style they prefer

Some people you approach will be delighted to be treated to lunch (make sure to take them somewhere decent; don't skimp out!). We wouldn't offer to take our mentor prospect to coffee; that isn't much of a treat. Find out what works best for them by asking what they would prefer: A nice sit-down lunch, drinks or coffee, a phone call?

Or perhaps they would prefer that you come to meet them at their office. Maybe they've been dying to see the new art gallery in town. Get a concrete answer to what THEY want. You can also make a suggestion if it's a little ambiguous, but remember: This is to treat THEM. They are doing you a favor by giving you invaluable inside travel information. Also, be sure to get any dietary restrictions if you're getting food.

Be clear about how much time you need

If the person that you are contacting is a busy person, they may not have time to make arrangements for lunch. Be clear that you are open to treating them to lunch only if their schedules allow for it. If not, ask them for 15 minutes of their time via phone, Skype, or FaceTime. The call here is crucial since you lose a lot of personality and human interaction through an email or DM.

Once you get a traveler talking about traveling, a topic that they are obviously quite passionate about, you'd be surprised as to how much people LOVE talking about themselves. The meeting could end up going on for hours, which is a bonus for you as a learning experience. Also, be extremely flexible, no one likes trying to schedule an appointment with someone with an overly complicated schedule.

Show your gratitude

Remember: Time is money. Even before you meet your potential mentor, let them know that you really appreciate that they are even considering speaking or meeting with you. Also, tell them that you would like to help them in any way possible in return. After you speak, we recommend that you follow up the meeting with a hand-written thank you note or card.

Once you lock in your meeting, the relationship isn't just done. Be sure to keep in touch with them at least once a month. It's important to maintain relationships with people regularly. You never know what crazy travel experience they may have down the line that you could find inspiration from, or maybe you can even travel together! The options are endless as long as you keep yourself open to the connection.

14

Day 14: REST

Get the streamers and balloons because you've officially made it through TWO WEEKS! You're absolutely KILLING it and you deserve your rest day. It's time to take a pause and soak in everything that you have accomplished thus far, and most importantly, relax.

Now, you have to make an honest promise to yourself that you are actually going to take the day off, not spend all this delicious relaxing time catching up on all the other travel tasks that you weren't able to finish throughout the week. Now is the time to veg out. How about finishing up that Netflix series you haven't gotten a chance to watch?

You know what they say, that while God was creating the world, even He took a rest on the 7th day. You don't need to be a religious person to get the gist of this.

We used to believe that we had absolutely no time to rest. We felt like we had so much to accomplish at all times, and the only way to do everything that we needed to do was to work long hours, seven days a week. We actually ended up accomplishing less this way because we would frequently have burned out periods where we were totally spent and ended up wasting more time. So, take a break. You deserve it.

These days, we make an effort to take at least two days off a week—usually Saturday and Sunday. By Monday, I'm actually excited to get back to work. Taking a few days off to recharge and rejuvenate gives you time to refresh your mindset and get excited to go back to work.

On this day off, it's a good time to reflect on how you are feeling about the challenge. You might still be feeling a bit overwhelmed by all the daily assignments, or you might feel super excited to see what Week 3 has in store. Remember, this 30-day challenge is meant to be fun, and as a future world traveler, it's important not to take life too crazy serious. There is no test at the end of this challenge or any stern teacher marking up scores of how well you did. If you missed a day, feel free to take an extra day to catch up.

Have you learned anything new? Maybe you had a revelation about yourself or some of your travel dreams and goals. Take a minute to jot down any new insights you learned from this past week and give yourself a huge pat on the back. Even if you didn't learn anything new, at least you are taking action to implement these steps towards travel.

30-DAY TRAVEL CHALLENGE

WEEK 2 REFLECTION

WHAT WAS YOUR BIGGEST INSPIRATION THIS WEEK?

_____

_____

_____

WHICH TITLES DID YOU PICK?

BOOK: _____

MOVIE: _____

WHAT GROUPS DID YOU JOIN AND WHY?

_____

_____

DESCRIBE YOUR TRAVEL FUND PLANS. HOW MUCH DO YOU NEED TO SAVE?

_____

_____

_____

_____

Use this reflection worksheet to help organize your thoughts:

30-DAY TRAVEL CHALLENGE

WEEK 2 REFLECTION

WHICH TRAVEL CONFERENCE DID YOU GO/PLAN ON GOING TO?

_____

_____

_____

WHAT WAS THE BIGGEST TAKEAWAY THAT YOU GOT FROM YOUR TRAVELER CONNECTION?

_____

_____

_____

_____

_____

_____

_____

_____

_____

III

Week 3: Taking actionable steps

15

Day 15: Do your research

Let's jump into Week 3. We are going to really dig into some actionable steps this week, and get into planning and preparing for your upcoming trip.

Today's challenge: Research, research, and research some more!

Now that you have decided where you want to go next, it's time to do your research.

There's a lot of information you'll need in order to have a successful trip. The more prepared you are in advance, the better and easier your trip will be. You're going to need to know how much plane tickets are, who are you traveling with, what hotels, and how much budget do you need for food, just to name a few. The clearer the plan that you make, the more likely it is to manifest!

We would recommend opening a Google Sheet within Google Docs for your research or using an Excel spreadsheet to record your data you're about to collect.

Click here for a free Google Travel Planning Sheet

Ready to get to work? Let's go!

Budgeting

You'll want to have a rough budget in mind before you start planning.

Ask yourself the following question: Are you looking to take a budget trip, staying in hostels and backpacking around Cambodia during its travel offseasons, or are you dreaming of a luxury vacation at the best hotels in Monaco? Come up with a rough number of what seems reasonable. We'll visit the budgeting portion again at the end of the research section.

Dates

Determine how long you want your trip to be and the tentative dates for your trip. For example, "I want 2 weeks in December, from December 1st to the 15th," or "Go on a weekend trip in March, from March 9th to March 13th."

Also, be sure you can actually take that time off. Will your work allow it? Can the kids stay with their grandma? Do you have pets that need sitting?

Documents

Will your trip be within the US, or will it be an international adventure? If you don't already have a passport, you'll need 4-6 weeks to apply for one and receive it in time for your trip out of the country. There are expedited services available that can get you set up with a new passport in as little as 2 weeks; however, this comes with an extra fee.

Also, are you planning on driving? Make sure that your driver's license is up to date if you're planning on renting a car. Check with the rental company if the country that you are visiting requires an international driving permit.

Find out if you need a visa to visit the country of your choice. Visas alone can get extremely complicated, so make sure to check your own country's requirements as well as that of the country you're traveling to. This can, ultimately, affect the dates that you're planning, so be ready for a bit of schedule shuffling.

Itinerary

Come up with a rough itinerary for your trip. If you are traveling across the ocean, you might want to plan a quieter first day for your trip to account for jet lag. Also, don't forget to incorporate your travel days if you're traveling a long distance. If you have specific restaurants, tours, excursions, and sights that you want to see, put them tentatively into your schedule. Are you hopping from city to city or visiting multiple countries during your trip? Map out how many days you plan to spend in each location.

For those of you who are looking for a less-customized itinerary, an all-inclusive tour might be an option to consider. When Kaila traveled to Vietnam, she signed up for a tour deal that was offered on Travel Pirates (as mentioned in Day 5). She paid about $1,244 for a 10-day trip from the south to the north of Vietnam, and all hotels, many meals, airfare, and local transport were taken care of. If you want to skip itinerary planning, she would recommend signing up for one of these tours.

If you are signing up for a tour package, your research and planning are done! However, many of you will prefer to plan out the trip on your own. Tours can be rigid and often have a regimented schedule with early mornings and late nights, and there's not a lot of freedom when it comes to exploring the sights you want to see. You don't get to choose where you are eating and travel with a group of strangers, so it's not for everyone.

When you are planning your trip, be sure to consider all the locations and accommodation you plan on staying at. Do you just want to stay in one hotel for the duration of the trip or do you want to see different parts of the area? Make a rough day-to-day plan of where you want to be and what you want to do. You don't want to pack your days too full and you also want to leave a bit of room for open exploring. You probably just want to plan one major excursion or activity a day and perhaps two sites or activities. Add all the options into your Google Sheet and list their details: Time and cost, etc.

Research airfare

You should book your airfare before you book anything else. Since most of us are planning our trips several months in advance, we recommend signing up for *Travel Pirates* or *Next Vacay*. Both are services that send out daily deals on airfare. *Travel Pirates* is totally free and *Next Vacay* charges a subscription of $20 a month, which is a worthy investment since you'll be saving hundreds or even thousands with this service. Also, input your flight and date details into a site such as *Airfarewatchdog* to get comparable costs of the plane tickets from different vendors.

Remember to sign up for any price notifications feature offered by these sites so you can see any changes in the cost of the plane tickets, which happen quite frequently and randomly. If you see a major deal or drop in the cost come up, be sure to snatch it. It's a bit like gambling; you don't want to wait for it to drop too low that you miss the opportunity. Buy tickets when they are reasonably priced for YOUR budget. Trying to play the market too much may cost you more in the long run.

Accommodation

Now that you've decided what areas you want to visit, it's time to check out where you're going to sleep at night. Most people see hotels as a place to literally store their bags while they're out and about exploring the area. On the contrary, some people look at hotels as a sanctuary, a home away from home. Decide what a hotel means for you on your trip. Do you want to stay in a major chain hotel, a boutique hotel or Airbnb? Explore all the options because your accommodation really does add to the overall travel experience.

If you really want to engage in a full travel experience and are on an exceptionally tight budget, consider doing a home-stay. This allows you to stay with a local family in their home and be fully immersed in the culture and language. It's an excellent way to truly "live like a local" while saving a little extra cash for excursions and souvenirs.

You can check out homestay opportunities here: https://www.homestay.com/

Research local travel

How are you going to get around the country after you land? We personally love Uber; it's available in many countries now, and is super easy to use, but you might want to consider even more affordable ways to travel if you are looking to save some money. Buses and trains are often a super-affordable option.

Will you be renting a car or bike to get around? Do the research and find out! Rail passes are also offered in many countries.

Insurance

Accidents can happen, and so it's best to be prepared for them. Consider if you want to get travel insurance for your journey. If you sign up for a travel credit card, you might already have coverage (that's coming up later in this challenge). Otherwise, you'll need to sign up for a travel insurance provider separately. Research your insurance provider costs and options for now, and later we'll revisit the topic of travel insurance after you've booked your plane tickets and hotel rooms. Also, don't forget to check to see if your health insurance covers overseas medical care.

Global Entry

If you are signing up for Global Entry directly, it costs just $100 for five years of coverage. Global Entry changed our lives, and we would never travel internationally without it! We got our Global Entry memberships for free with our Chase Sapphire travel credit cards (more on travel credit cards on Day 20). You can apply for Global Entry here.

One time, we were traveling to India together. Kaila was already set with Global Entry, but Kiki didn't have it for that trip. Low and behold, Kaila breezed through US customs. There was no line at all, and with Global Entry, you don't need to be interviewed by a U.S. customs officer. All you do is waive the receipt that you grab at one of the automated kiosks (that look like little TSA vending machines) and you're all set! After you get your luggage from baggage claim, you also get to go through a separate, much faster line to exit. VIP ACCESS! All in all, Kaila arrived at the connecting flight an hour before, and Kiki just barely made the connecting flight, jumping through a nightmare of hoops without Global Entry.

If you're thinking this was a pretty hectic research day, you're not alone. We know it can feel a bit overwhelming, but it can also be a lot of fun exploring and planning the details of your trip. Doesn't it feel good to have a skeleton of a trip laid out? Getting super clear about your trip will start to make your trip go from a pipe dream to a tangible reality.

Great work! Give yourself a huge pat on the back because you've got one of the toughest parts of this book DONE!

16

Day 16: Set up a budget

Today's challenge: Plan for your trip by exploring all costs

Feeling like you could have a degree in science after all that research? You're probably not wrong!

Now that you've done your research it's time to set up a formal budget. There's nothing that sucks more than coming back from a dream-worthy vacation to have debt that takes months or even years to pay off. How can you even plan your next vacation with that dark cloud hanging over your head?

By the way, we used to have problems with credit cards and still love to spend money. We totally understand if you are feeling some resistance and angst to this part already. Even though we're not the biggest fans of budgeting, just stick with us here; We promise that the rewards of budgeting outweigh the pain of doing the nitty-gritty, number-crunching work.

By now, you should be pretty clear on your destination and you've done some research into accommodation options and plane tickets. Let's dive into putting together a ... dun dun dun ... drum roll, please ... formal budget!

Yesterday, you did all the research into major expenses. Now it's time to build out a budget, preferably with a spreadsheet. Spreadsheets will make it easier to visualize your budget in an organized fashion and run quick calculations so you don't have to whip out the calculator, pen, and paper.

Here are some other incidental expenses that we didn't cover in the last day that you should be adding into your budget:
- cash/souvenirs
- airport fees: Parking/Uber, checked bags, food
- tips
- internet (Wifi hotspots)
- phone/SIM card
- immunizations
- visas

Sample budget

We are using a real example for a previous trip that Kaila took to Thailand from February 21st to February 29th. For this trip, she used travel-hacking techniques to book business class tickets. The round-trip flights were from Los Angeles to Penang. She went on a couple of fun local tours and excursions. Also, she used her Hyatt credit card for 2 free luxury hotel nights, while the other 4 nights she chose a beautiful Airbnb stay for $80 a night.

Here's the breakdown:

Round-trip flights to Phuket using credit card hacking techniques: **$475.98**. Kaila just searched *Skyscanner* and found some killer tickets at $743 a person. So if you paid full price for tickets, it's possible to score 2 economy class tickets for $1486.

8 nights lodging in Phuket (2 nights free with Hyatt reward card): **$480**

Phi Phi Island snorkeling tour: $107 per person, **$214** total

Transportation for 2 people: tuk tuks and taxis: **$200**

Day cruise and buffet: $114 per person, **$228** total

Food for 9 days (Kaila only eats local food while traveling, which is much cheaper than eating at the Westernized restaurants or hotel restaurants): $20 per person per day, $40 a day. **$720** total (not including alcohol)

Money for incidentals, shopping, souvenirs, etc.: $300 per person, **$600** total

Wifi hotspot rental: **$60**

Uber to and from the airport: **$80**

Tips: **$100**

Total with travel hacking for 2 people: **$3,157.98**

Total without travel hacking for 2 people: **$4,168**

Using travel hacking tactics, the total for two people for the entire trip is $3,157.98, which is quite a steal for a 9-day tropical getaway. Let's round it up to $3,160 for convenience. That's a budget of $1,580 per person for the entire trip. If you're just saving up for your portion of the trip in the next 6 months, you would need to put aside $263 a month to save up for the trip. If you're planning for a trip next year, all you need to set aside is $131.50 a month.

If you're thinking, "Wait, I don't have that kind of money to save," don't get too concerned yet. Budgeting your monthly finances is tricky, but definitely feasible.

Tomorrow, we'll cover ways that you can actually save for your budget, so keep reading on and don't get discouraged!

As extra motivation, you can post your travel savings goal up on the refrigerator as a friendly reminder to continue to save daily. Refrigerator notes are the best, too, since you're always heading there for a mental break or snack; your mind is refreshed and ready to process new information. The reminder is a great way to instill the mindset of saving when you are refreshed and ready to take it in.

Also, while you're traveling, you'll want to track your spending so that you make sure that you don't go over budget! We love to use Mint and the Mint app, but there is a plethora of great money tracking and budgeting apps available. Mint also has an awesome countdown feature that shows your progress towards your savings goal that we love and recommend.

Now that you have your travel budget ready to go, make sure to add it to your main budget as a line item.

If you aren't smart with your money (like we used to be), it's a great time to get financially fit! We're not going to delve into personal finance tips here; it's just not that kind of book. However, we would recommend picking up the book *The Total Money Makeover: Classic Edition: A Proven Plan for Financial Fitness, by Dave Ramsey* here to give your finances a killer overhaul.

It's important to be fully aware of your spending at all times. This means checking your bank accounts and statements like a hawk. As someone who had suffered from some serious credit card debt, Kaila being on top of any overcharges or extra spending/saving is extremely important in order for her to stay within budget.

An extremely helpful tool for tracking spending is the phone app called Mint, as we briefly just mentioned. This app is a seriously high-powered tool that allows you to directly connect your bank accounts and view your financial health as a whole. Also, you can input your spending, save receipts, view your income, and plan your budgets by category. It's truly an incredible app that can lift a huge daily financial planning weight off your shoulders. Plus, you can use it anytime and anywhere with your smartphone.

For those of you who prefer to do it the semi-old fashioned way or who just aren't fans of phone apps, we've provided you with a budgeting spreadsheet here.

Free Download: TRAVEL BUDGET WORKSHEET

Designing a healthy travel budget is an essential part of your travel experience. If you're prepared ahead of time, you can avoid some serious issues of being ill-prepared overseas. After all, it would be the ultimate nightmare if you didn't have enough cash to make it back from your trip to the Andes.

Remember, budgeting may take some time. This is a 30-day challenge, but don't feel obligated to take out a bunch of credit cards that you can't afford just so you can travel within these 30 days. Do what's healthy for your financial health in the long run. If it takes time to budget out the right amount of money for your travel, TAKE THE TIME. Finances should never be rushed. Financial decisions should always be made with a sound and conservative attitude. With the right amount of time and planning, you'll be well on your way to a successful and incredible dream vacation.

So, now that you've got your travel fund squared away, tomorrow we'll explore ideas on how to kickstart your travel fund.

17

Day 17: Kickstart your travel fund

Today's challenge: How can you save even more for travel?

What a productive week this has been already! If you're diligently staying on schedule, you've already accomplished a huge amount. Are you getting super excited about your upcoming trip? Good! Keep up that excitement level and passion—that feeling is what's going to drive you out that door and to the airport.

Today, we are going to brainstorm ideas on how to kickstart your travel fund and get you one step closer to your dream destination!

Here are some ideas on how to score some extra change for your travel fund:

How to save a little extra coin

Now that you've established your budget for the trip and set your savings goals, it's time to start building your travel fund. Could you spare 5%, 10%, or more of your paycheck each month to go into your travel fund? You can even start by just adding $5 into the fund right now, just to get started. You'll be surprised to see how fast your travel savings account grows as long as you are depositing into it regularly, no matter what the amount.

Your morning cup o' Joe

Did you know that you can spend, on average, $50-80 per month on coffee alone? If you're a huge fan of Starbucks, you might want to start brewing your morning Joe at home. Or, you can consider a cheaper alternative if you really need your morning fix. McDonald's coffee is a great way to get your caffeine in, or even hit up the gas station. It's no designer coffee but think about the time spent on the beach in the Bahamas. Perhaps "Starbs" can wait. Check out this nifty little coffee savings calculator: http://www.hughchou.org/calc/coffee.cgi

Eating out

Are you the type that loves to buy lunch at work? Whether it's for convenience or flavor, unpaid work lunches can add up. Even if you're buying a cheapo for $5 a day, that's $25 a week, or $100 a month! Consider preparing a brown paper bag lunch box like the ones Mom used to pack you. Mama always knows best!

Also, you can even cut costs in how often you go out. We understand that there's nothing better than getting happy hour with your co-workers after a long day of work, or even treating yourself to your favorite restaurant. However, if you can elimi-nate one or two days of eating out, that can ultimately save you around $30 a week, or $120 a month.

Transportation

Could you bike to the office or to your errands instead of driving a car? It's better for the environment and also great for exercise! If you're in walking distance, take a stroll to work or even carpool with your co-workers. Also, if you live in the city, public transportation is an excellent alternative to driving.

Get rid of the cable!

Let's face it, how much TV do you NEED to watch? By getting rid of your cable TV service, this could definitely save another $1,000 a year or more. Netflix is so inexpensive (around $120 a year) and YouTube has tons of free videos and movies, also.

Utility bills

Depending on where you live, maybe you can sacrifice that good ole heater in the winter times and add an extra layer when you're indoors. Turn on the fan in the summertime instead of using the air conditioner. Not using the air conditioner or heater can save quite a bit of money. Just pretend you're exploring the Amazon river in a hot, humid climate (slightly kidding here). Also, try doing fewer loads of laundry and consolidating all your clothing into one load, instead.

Cancel your gym membership

If you're really not using the gym as much as you'd like, consider cutting out your gym membership. There are tons of free workouts available on YouTube, which you can do from the comfort of your own home. Kaila spent a month working out to one of her favorite channels on YouTube in preparation for a trip to Fiji and was very happy with the results!

Vices

This part is a bit tricky but can be extremely expensive. Alcohol and cigarettes can cost you a pretty penny. Think about how much alcohol you consume. If you have a beer a day ($5), you can be looking at $35 a week—$140 a month. If you can't cut them out entirely, try ordering one less glass of wine with your meal or smoking fewer cigarettes per day.

Side jobs

Can you get a part-time job? Could you spend a few or more hours a week dog-walking, bartending, waiting tables, bookkeeping, remote data entry, selling your creations on Etsy? What we did for extra cash is we first made a list of every skill that we had, from the ridiculous to the legit. For example, Kaila's list included: Cat petting, biking, sleeping, public relations, and event planning.

To start, just take out a sheet of paper and brainstorm at least 100 things that you know how to do. Then, go to Craigslist and see what kind of odd jobs are out there. We also love this awesome side job resource on Reddit: https://www.reddit.com/r/personalfinance/wiki/sideincome

Your main vein job

Maybe it's time to ask for a raise or put in a few hours of overtime. It's always a good idea to submit a performance appraisal, especially if you've been loyal to the company and have been performing well. Also, after you've reviewed your skill sets, maybe it's time to find a new job that can accommodate your travel (only if this is actually possible, of course).

Sell your stuff!

Most of us have tons of stuff gathering dust deep in our closet. These are things in our lives that we are holding on to but don't really need. We've both had dresses in our closets that we hadn't worn for years but held on to just in case the occasion arose that we might've worn them again.

A great way to kickstart your travel fund is to put up your items for sale on Craigslist, Poshmark, or eBay. You could also host a garage sale but it takes a few more steps (seeing if you need a permit, posting signs around the neighborhood, finding a location if you can't use your lawn, etc.).

Tax refund/work bonus

Have a tax refund or work bonus coming up? Put it right into your travel fund to get you started!

You'll be surprised how effective it is to budget your lifestyle. Once you get into the groove of things, the gratification of saving is actually more rewarding than the stuff that you used to collect and consume. These are financial changes that we decided to make in our lives, initially for travel. However, we found that it ended up making our entire lifestyles better, easier, and more enjoyable.

You don't have to go and do all of these things at once. Take it one step at a time. It's not easy to get a raise just like that or to sell all of your extra clothes. As long as you stick to the course and work at it each day, you WILL be successful. Your goals are on the horizon, figuratively and literally, because that's what we'll be covering tomorrow.

18

Day 18: Set goals

Today's challenge: Set one travel goal (or two or
three, whatever you're comfortable with. Just set at
least one!)

We hope you aren't getting overwhelmed; this is a heavy-duty
action week! Can you believe that it's already Day 18? It's crazy
how time flies!

Today, we are working on a crucial step for making your travel
dreams a reality: Goal setting! For the purpose of this exercise,
goal setting means crystal clear, numerical, timed, and defined
goals, *not* vague ideas like, "I want to travel more."

There was a fascinating study conducted at the Harvard MBA
School in 1979, as detailed in *What They Don't Teach You at Harvard
Business School* by Mark McCormack. Out of a group of clearly
exceptional high-achievers, only 3% had written down clear
goals of what they intended to accomplish. Ten years later, they
interviewed this same set of people again and found that this

3% of the class was earning ten times as much as the other 97% combined. Can you imagine how much farther ahead in the game you could possibly be if you made a habit of writing down your goals?

Here are some steps to take in goal setting:

Decide on what you want to accomplish and write it down

Let's use the example of, "I want to travel more." Now, what does this mean for you? 5 and 10-year goals are a little more difficult to conceive, especially in this fast-paced world where technology is changing so rapidly. So, let's just start with a 1-year goal. Also, let's make it a monetary goal since it's a more tangible way to quantify an abstract idea. For example, Kaila's goal is to save $230 a month to travel to Okinawa Island in Japan in October (say it's in 6 months). Using the budgeting techniques that you have learned in the previous days, you can now break down the goal into tangible, bite-sized monthly money savings goals.

Tip: We prefer setting almost outlandish goals for ourselves; ones that we have no idea how we are going to achieve. The reason for this is that even if you shoot for the stars and miss, you are still getting pretty high up in the sky. Set goals so high that even if you make it halfway there it'll be a big success. By doing this, it pushes you to stretch yourself to your outer limits. Also, it's so much more exciting and motivating to have a huge goal in mind.

Set a definite date for the goal completion

The reason we do this is because part of setting a goal is making a plan of action to make it happen. Setting a date is always a step towards creating a firmer commitment to the goal. It also helps you be able to quantify your goal and break it down into smaller steps.

Bookend it

This means telling someone you trust about the goal and letting them know when you have accomplished it. When you tell someone else about your goal, it makes you more accountable and helps you commit even more to achieve the goal. Also, it helps to have a cheerleader throughout your process.

Strategize

You're going to need a plan of action for your goal. Break the goal into smaller, easier steps and visualize your path to arrive at the finish line. After you set your 1-year goal, it helps to breakdown the goal into even smaller sets, like 6-month goals, 1-month goals, weekly goals and then daily goals. So for Kaila, the 1-year goal would be, "I want my business to gross $200,000 by January 1st, 2017." That means that she should be hitting $100,000 by June 1st, 2016; $16,666 a month, $757 a day (factoring a 5-day work week), and $94 an hour.

A quick tip: Take it one day at a time. Looking at the overall goal can sometimes be overwhelming. It's good to keep your major goals in the back of your mind, but in the day-to-day process, just do your best and take it easy! If you don't hit your daily, weekly, or monthly goal today, that's ok. It's important to set goals, but it's even more important to enjoy the process along the way.

You can even just set the goal of finishing this 30-day challenge in 30 days. The point of this exercise is just to think about setting goals for various areas of your life. Write down those goals for the necessary clarity!

30-DAY TRAVEL CHALLENGE

GOALS WORKSHEET

WHAT DO YOU WANT TO ACCOMPLISH WITH YOUR
TRAVELS IN 1 YEAR?

_____

_____

_____

WHAT IS THE DATE YOU WILL FINISH YOUR GOALS?

DATE:

WHO IS HOLDING YOU ACCOUNTABLE FOR YOUR GOALS?

_____

WHAT ARE THE ACTIONABLE STEPS YOU ARE GOING TO
TAKE TO ACHIEVE THESE GOALS?

_____

_____

_____

_____

_____

_____

30-DAY TRAVEL CHALLENGE

GOALS WORKSHEET

WHY DO YOU WANT TO ACHIEVE THESE GOALS?

_____

_____

_____

WHAT ARE YOUR TRAVEL GOALS FOR THE NEXT FIVE YEARS?

_____

_____

_____

_____

_____

_____

_____

_____

_____

_____

_____

19

Day 19: Learn about travel hacking

Today's challenge: Find out if travel hacking is for you

Finally, the moment you've all been waiting for ... TRAVEL HACKING (our favorite).

We are absolutely obsessed with travel hacking. We are not earning a million dollars a year, so we are not comfortable spending $3,000 of our own hard-earned cash on a one-way international business class flight. We might not even want to spend that cash unless we were billionaires; it just seems like such a frivolous expense, especially if there's a way to get it for a fraction of the price.

Even if you don't have any desire to take business class flights, you can use travel hacking techniques to score free flights and hotel rooms around the world.

Our relationship with travel hacking wasn't always flowers and dandelions. We stayed away from travel hacking for years because we used to have problems with credit cards. Kaila signed up for her first credit card on her college campus at just 17-years-old. At that age, it was just like free money to her, and she promptly went out and bought a pair of $500 Prada platforms (hey, they were friggin adorable!) By the time she left college, she was $15,000 in debt and had nothing to show for it.

It was so bad that she even joined Debtors Anonymous, which eventually helped her to clear her debt, 100%. The program requires 100% abstinence from credit cards and she was completely credit card-free and debt-free for 10 years. However, it was frustrating because so many of the top travel bloggers that she followed were travel hacking their way to her dream destinations, and she was just at home watching.

It took a lot of soul-searching, but she finally signed up for her first travel credit card several years ago. She now has about 8 different travel credit cards, but she maintains all of them at a zero balance. We use the credit cards purely for the purposes of travel hacking, and anything that we spend on the credit cards is paid off **immediately**.

If you doubt your capabilities to rigorously maintain a zero balance on your credit cards, we recommend skipping today's and tomorrow's content. If you already currently have credit card debt, skip these two days, too. You should only travel hack if you have zero credit card debt, so pay off your credit cards before you attempt travel hacking.

Some say that it's possible to travel hack without credit cards. But in our opinion, it's not really worth your time investment, unless you are using credit cards. This is because credit cards offer huge points bonuses when you sign up. 50,000 and 100,000 point sign-up bonuses are super common, and you only need around 150,000 points for a round trip business class flight from Los Angeles to Asia. Plus, you'll need far fewer points if you are traveling domestically or not traveling across an ocean for your trip!

We prefer to use our miles for business class and first class flights, only because it makes flying an enjoyable experience that we actually look forward to. However, if you are just using points to redeem domestic economy flights, you can easily be on your way to taking a free trip in a month or two. It takes a bit more time to accumulate points for a premium trip—on average, it takes us about 4 months to accumulate enough points for one international business class ticket. We are very conservative about travel hacking, and only sign up for one new credit card once a month.

For today, just research some travel hacking blogs and find out what it's all about. Our favorite blogs are, *One Mile at a Time*, and *The Points Guy*. If you are serious about travel hacking, subscribe to their email newsletters; they send out daily emails about what's the latest and greatest in travel hacking.

Here are some further travel hacking resources for you:
- Great resource page on travel hacking
- Top travel hacking blogs
- Award Travel 101® Facebook group

(Read on to the end of the book for an interview with Richard

Kerr, the founder of the Award Travel 101® Facebook group).

We're going to cover how to sign up for travel credit cards tomorrow, but below are a few methods of travel hacking without using credit cards:

Watch for special offers

We sign up for travel brand newsletters because they often have featured points offers that are not found on an airline's website. This could be triple miles on a selected route or as simple as Starwood's recent promotion. We signed up for their newsletter and got 250 SPG (Starwood's Preferred Guest) points. American Airlines once gave away 1,000 points for installing a shopping toolbar into your web browser. These bonuses don't go into the high tens of thousands, but you can earn some points for little effort. Smaller points add up, so be sure to take advantage of these opportunities.

Use airline shopping portals

All airlines, hotels, and travel brands have preferred merchants. These companies—ranging from clothing retailers to sporting good stores to office supply businesses and everything in between—partner with airlines' special shopping malls. By ordering online through an airline's website, you can earn additional points.

For example, we originally registered for Netflix through American Airlines' website because it gave an additional 5,000 miles in their point system. We also went to shop on Target's website via Chase's online shopping mall and earned three points per dollar spent. We did household shopping online with Kmart via American Airlines' portal and received nine miles per dollar spent.

You can use Evreward or Cashback Monitor to discover the current best deals across various programs. Simply type in the merchant or product you want, and they will compile a list of bonuses that points programs are offering at that moment; that way, you can get the best bang for your buck.

(Outside the United States, Canada has two shopping portals: Shop.ca and The Aeroplan eStore. If you are in the UK, there is also a shopping portal at British Airways' eStore).

Dining rewards programs

Just like shopping portals, many airlines also have dining rewards programs. First, you sign up with your frequent flier number, register your credit card, and get extra points when you dine at participating restaurants in the airline's network (which rotate throughout the year). Join one of the programs in the rewards network (they run all the dining programs) and you can get five miles per dollar spent once you became a "VIP member," which happens after 12 dines. If you get those 12 under your belt (so to speak) early in the year, you'll be getting five points per dollar spent for the rest of the year. FREE MONEY!

Choose an alliance

When you're playing the travel hacking points and miles game, you should choose an alliance/airline to focus on. Ultimately, you should focus on earning miles on American Airlines and not fly different domestic airlines every single time because you can't transfer miles between certain airlines. You can't transfer your Delta Airlines points that you diligently accrued for that sweet deal to London on American Airlines (bummer).

When flying internationally, you should focus on the alliance that your chosen airline is part of. There are three major alliances: Star Alliance, SkyTeam, and Oneworld. For this example, American Airlines is a member of the Oneworld alliance. If you're flying to Asia, you'll want to choose Cathay Pacific (Oneworld) over Air China (Star Alliance). The reason for this is because Oneworld points earned are transferable to other airline partners in the same alliance.

In the movie *Up in the Air*, George Clooney's character said, "I don't do anything if it doesn't benefit my miles account." Think like that. Your bank account will be thanking you later.

Again, we want to remind you to only commit to travel hacking with a credit card if you are capable of paying off your balances 100% of the time. This is only for expenditures that you know you can afford. Don't start going crazy trying to collect miles and end up in a debt that you can't bear.

However, if you are financially responsible, this is an excellent way to be able to afford travel. After all, it's free money waiting to be spent. Why not take advantage?

20

Day 20: Sign up for a travel credit card

Today's challenge: Explore all the travel credit card options available

Kaila recently took a trip to Thailand with the two business class flights and two luxury hotel nights completely comped. It took me about 8 months to earn all of these rewards, which is much longer than average. Her boyfriend at the time didn't want to travel hack, nor wanted to sign up for a travel credit card, so she had to earn enough points for two people to take the trip. If you follow a similar path, you can earn enough for a long-haul international business class trip in about 4 months. It'll take even less time if you are just looking for round-trip international economy tickets, and even less time if you are just looking for a domestic vacay. The possibilities are endless!

Again, and we're going to keep nailing this in, we want to stress that **we don't recommend signing up for a travel credit card unless you have ZERO unsecured debt.** Don't sign up for a new credit card until you pay off all the balances on any of your current credit cards. And don't make purchases with your newfound credit card that you can't afford. Period.

When signing up for a credit card with a bonus offer, there is usually a minimum spend requirement averaging around $3,000-5,000, which you usually have three months to reach. It might sound like a lot but we just simply put all our expenses onto the credit card that we are currently trying to earn bonus miles on. Groceries, utilities, anything that we can put on there. One caveat is that we pay off the credit cards immediately, as soon as the transaction shows up on the statement. This is super easy to do via online banking. Also, we never sign up for more than one new credit card at a time because we don't want to risk not hitting the minimum spend and thus missing out on the bonus! It usually takes us about 2 months to hit the minimum spend and earn the bonus, and we usually sign up for a new credit card immediately.

Most of these credit cards also have an annual fee, which is often waived the first year. The fee is usually around $100 for the average card, up to $550 for cards with tons of perks like the ultra-ritzy American Express Platinum Travel Card.

Other perks of signing up for a travel credit card are that many of them include travel insurance, no foreign transaction fees while traveling, baggage check-in fees waivers, and more. Cards like the Platinum Card from American Express and the Chase Sapphire Reserve also offer airport lounge access and credits for Global Entry/TSA PreCheck.

We recommend reading websites like The Points Guy and

One Mile at a Time to find out the latest and greatest sign-up bonuses and details for each credit card.

Here is the case study for the process that Kaila used when booking her two flights to Thailand

Using points, she booked two round-trip business class tickets to Bangkok on Eva Air worth $3041.50 a piece.

All the bonuses she signed up for ranged from 75,000 points to 100,000 points. She used Chase and AMEX points to earn her miles:

1. Signed up for the Chase Sapphire card: 100,000 sign up bonus
2. Signed up for the Chase Ink card: 75,000 sign up bonus
3. Signed up for the Chase Reserve card: 100,000 sign up bonus
4. Signed up for the AMEX Business Platinum: 75,000 sign up bonus

Total miles earned with credit card sign up bonuses: 350,000

For the two business class plane tickets, she spent 317,000 miles on United Airlines and Aeroplan.

Total Money Spent: Airline taxes on two tickets: $72.99 each = $145.98

Kaila didn't want to figure out how to book the awards plane tickets since it's a time consuming matter, so she just hired BookYourAward to find the best awards tickets for her. (You can get additional help on finding awards tickets on Facebook groups like https://www.facebook.com/groups/awardtravel101 or Flyertalk.com).

Book your award service fee for booking two business class tickets: $165 each = $330

TOTAL SPENT: $475.98

She also signed up for the Hyatt credit card which comes with 2 free nights at any of their properties. Some properties, such as the Park Hyatt Maldives Hadahaa, run at over $1,000 a night, so you'll be getting extremely great value if you choose the right hotel for your redemptions.

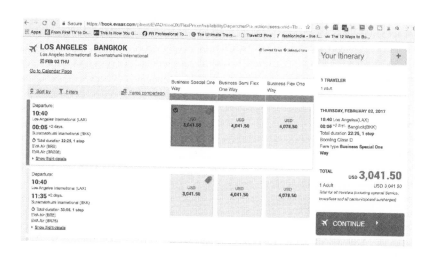

Here's a screenshot of how much one ticket would have cost if she had paid full price:

Round-trip Business Class tickets on Eva Air: $3,041.50 a piece = $6,083

Two nights at the Grand Hyatt Taipei: $223.15 a night = $446.30
TOTAL VALUE: $6,529.30
The most current and best credit card offers are listed here:

Remember, the sooner you sign up for your credit card, the sooner you can start budgeting your expenses and accruing more points. If you are financially sound and ready to sign up, do it today. Don't put this on the back burner, because you are losing out on points each day you procrastinate this task.

Choose the right credit card for your budgeting. Just because a credit card has an incredible deal doesn't mean it's the right one for you.

If you've gotten this far, you are already a top tier travel planner. Pat yourself on the back, because you've got a day of rest ahead!

21

Day 21: REST

It's been a highly productive week! We hope you feel super motivated with everything that you have accomplished, and are excited with all the progress that you have made so far. You've already set a strong foundation with your mindset, planned your travel, and even set a budget! That's HUGE!

You might be feeling exhausted after putting forth so much travel planning effort this week. Luckily, today is a day of rest and a chance for a little "you time."

Today, let's take the time out to just think about any struggles that you faced this week. What was difficult about this last week? Did you discover some tricky financial situations that you didn't know you were in?

Also, reflect on what brought you to sign up for this 30-day travel challenge in the first place. What do you plan to do in the future to make sure that all your travel dreams come true? Have you found any useful tools that will help you develop more of a frequent traveler lifestyle? What are your goals for the upcoming week?

We absolutely love this quote:

"Twenty years from now you will be more disappointed by the things that you didn't do than by the ones you did do. So throw off the bowlines. Sail away from the safe harbor. Catch the trade winds in your sails. Explore. Dream. Discover." —Mark Twain

It's so true! Life is all about experiences and sharing those same experiences with the people you love or meeting new people along the way. When all is said and done, all you have left are your memories, relationships, and experiences. It's important to invest in these and pave a beautiful life that you deserve. The right time is now. Stop waiting for your dreams to become a reality!

Feel free to use this reflection sheet below as an outline to organize your thoughts:

We're almost two-thirds of the way through this travel challenge. Can you believe it? Let's go!

30-DAY TRAVEL CHALLENGE

WEEK 3 REFLECTION

NAME ONE MAJOR FIND FROM YOUR RESEARCH THIS WEEK.

_____

_____

_____

WERE YOU ABLE TO SAY WITHIN YOUR PLANNED BUDGET?

_____

_____

DESCRIBE 3 WAYS YOU ARE ACTIVELY SAVING TOWARDS YOUR TRAVEL GOALS.

_____

_____

_____

WHAT IS YOUR FAVORITE TRAVEL HACKING TACTIC? IF YOU DIDN'T GET A CREDIT CARD, DESCRIBE ONE WAY YOU ARE WORKING TOWARDS DECREASING YOUR DEBTS.

_____

_____

_____

IV

Week 4: Crossing the finish line

22

Day 22: Write a bucket list

Today's challenge: Explore your wildest travel dreams!

We are on the final week of the 30-Day Travel Challenge and you are absolutely killing it!

In Week 1, we set the foundation for traveling more, exploring some of our belief systems and exploring our own cities.

In Week 2, we looked for inspiration all around us to motivate us to get off our butts and travel more.

Week 3, we really dug our heels in and got into the nitty-gritty of travel planning. We actually mapped out our trips by doing the research, got our budgets in place and even put a bit of money in our travel funds! This week, we are going to bring it all home by having fun and thinking outside of the box and exploring travel concepts we may have never even imagined.

We are going to learn about how seasoned travelers explore alternative methods of traveling contrary to the average traveler.

Have you seen the movie, *The Bucket List* starring Morgan Freeman and Jack Nicholson? If you haven't, here's a quick synopsis:

The Bucket List is a movie about two terminally-ill cancer patients who are complete strangers, whose only link is their desires to fulfill the rest of their short lives. The odd couple make an epic list of all of the things that they would like to do before they die, causing them to go on an adventure of a lifetime and build an unbreakable bond and friendship. After watching the movie you learn that happiness is found by living life to the fullest and ensuring that you never let your fears or doubts get in the way of doing so.

Taking the time out to write this bucket list can help to guide you towards a life of deeper meaning and purpose. It may change your perspective from living life as a "human doing" to experiencing life as a "human being."

To start your journey of travel self-exploration, we highly recommend defining what the phrase "bucket list" means to you. Is a bucket list a representation of a narrow list of activities that you will complete later, somewhere down the road, when most of your life is over and you are finally retired? Or, does a bucket list take on a broader meaning for you? Maybe it's an opportunity where you can start to live life in the now and not in the future? Or perhaps you'll find that your definition exists somewhere between these two.

Once you have defined your personal meaning of what a bucket list is, get out your piece of paper, journal, computer, tablet or smartphone and record your vision of the travel experiences that you wish to fulfill. To bring color and form to your vision, we highly recommend incorporating the following steps into your brainstorming process:

Purpose

Establish what it is you want out of your travel life. For each of these "wants," assign the "why" behind what you want. Determining your "whys" helps to create traction for each goal, and allows you to reflect on whether each goal is truly an experience you must have.

Sometimes, experience may seem like just a good idea. Experiences that fall under the category of a good idea may fail to materialize since you don't have a compelling reason to fulfill that intended vision.

Direction

Determine who exactly you see yourself as, as an outcome of your travel experiences. In other words, who is the individual you wish to be at the end of your life? What does this person look like? Sound like? What are this person's value systems? What knowledge would they have gained? What friends would they have? How are they loved by their family? Ask as many questions as you can at this juncture, then work backwards from your ideal image of yourself. Pinpoint activities, experiences, and belief systems that will be the building blocks to help you arrive at the destination you have in your mind's eye.

Priority

Once you have plotted out a timeline based on working backwards from your end-vision, you will need to determine immediate horizons, mid-term horizons, and long-term horizons. Your horizons are the actions you will possibly be able to take during the time frame you set.

For example, your immediate horizons could happen tomorrow or next month. Your mid-term horizons could be over the course of the next 5 years. Long-term horizons could even be until you retire. Pick the timeline that best describes the time you want to spend traveling.

Then, within each of your time horizons, you will need to determine which goals take on the most significance for you. In other words, which bucket list items get your blood moving as you stare at your ideas on paper? Essentially, you want to front-load those goals that truly inspire you and that you strongly believe you can fulfill within the immediate time horizon.

Why? Because it is vital that you develop a consistent pattern of completing your goals in order to build a sustainable commitment to your bucket list over the years to come.

A wise man once said, "You are what you do, not what you say you'll do."

By this point, you should have a strong framework of where you are currently, where you would like to be in the future, the "whys" that will drive you to reach your goals, and your established time horizons. However, you may find it's still difficult to clearly picture your future life, even after all that brainstorming.

To help you explore all the aspects of life you would like to assign to your bucket list, please find below some thought-provoking questions to ask yourself:

1. How would you like to be remembered? Years from now, when stories are being told by your descendants at family gatherings, what distinction(s) would you like to hold in your family line?
2. What if you were to die tomorrow? What would you wish you could do before you die?
3. What would you do if you had unlimited time, money, and resources?
4. What have you always wanted to do but have not done yet?
5. Are there any countries, places or locations you've wanted to visit but never made the time to do so? (We know this applies to you, or else you wouldn't be reading this book!)
6. What are your biggest goals and dreams?
7. Who do you want to meet before you die?
8. What achievements do you want to have?
9. What experiences do you want to have?
10. What activities or skills do you want to learn or try out?
11. What would you like to experience while traveling with other people; the people you love, your family, and your friends?
12. Lastly, what do you need to do to lead a life of the absolute greatest meaning to you?

Here's a page out of Kaila's personal travel bucket list:
1. Fly in the Singapore Suites from the United States to Asia
2. Stay at an overwater bungalow suite in the Maldives

3. Swim with the pigs in Nassau
4. Go on a cruise to Antarctica
5. Go to Tashirojima, aka Cat Island, in Japan
6. Eat at René Redzepi's Noma, wherever it's currently at in the world
7. Ride on a camel in Egypt
8. Swim with the manatees in Florida or Mexico

3 reasons why you should have your own bucket list

1. If you tend to procrastinate, your list will help remind you that you're on a timeline and that you have got to keep going to pursue your travel dreams.
2. Your dreams can sometimes seem a little outlandish when they're swirling around in your braincase. However, when you write them down and make them tangible, they suddenly seem a lot more realistic.
3. People get overwhelmed sometimes when planning doesn't go their way. This leads to frustration and unfulfilled dreams. Writing down your bucket list is an easy and excellent way to establish your travel goals. It's so much easier to operate when you're working with an outline with an end goal.

Creating your own bucket list is essential for planning your travels because so many people go through life feeling unhappy due to life prevented them from living out their dream experiences. Don't be that person. Your bucket list will be the anchor for you to stay the course in your travel experiences, and in your life overall.

** We love bucket lists so much that we actually started a National Bucket List Day! We would love to have you celebrate with us on May 21st, 2019 and share your bucket list goals on social media with us at **#NationalBucketListDay**. Scroll to the end of the book for more details!

23

Day 23: Explore vagabonding

Today's challenge: Explore the idea of being a full-time traveler

Are you a vagabond at heart? A vagabond is someone who travels from place to place with no permanent residence, making a home wherever the road takes him/her.

This can be wildly romantic and appealing, especially if you're the type with an insatiable urge for exploring. Many of the travelers we've met along our journeys are vagabonds or digital nomads.

In the book *Vagabonding,* Rolf Potts teaches that traveling is not just reserved for the wealthy. He delves into the unconventional lifestyle of making money while you travel and traveling while you make money. It's a true travelers dream, and he makes that vision absolutely real for those that find the lifestyle intriguing.

If this is making your inner self scream, "THAT'S ME," then you're in for some luck. We're about to dive head-first into all the details of vagabonding.

How to be a vagabond

Work overseas

Could you explore what you do for work in a different country? Does the company that you work for have overseas offices? There are a few things you can do for research:

Search job boards in your target city

Reach out to different expat groups, on Facebook or online, and inquire about job opportunities.

Explore teaching English or Spanish overseas. The pay can often be pretty decent. First, you'll want to decide on the region you want to teach English in because different countries and regions require different qualifications. For example, it pays incredibly well to teach in the Middle East, but you'll also need a higher education and certifications to qualify for a job.

Join the Peace Corps. Not only are you helping the world, but you are also receiving a small stipend for your good deeds! The Peace Corps provides you with living arrangements, and medical and dental training while you are serving, in addition to a stipend for living. It's free to apply and to participate, and if you've completed two years of service, they'll even provide you with $8,000 as an aid to help you transition back to living at home. They also cover the cost of your transportation from your home to your assigned location.

Here are some resources to help you explore more deeply into working abroad:

Alliances Abroad. This amazing organization assists in helping people work overseas, as well as with living arrangements. They connect employees and interns with companies who are in need of work.

Bunac. Explore work, volunteer, or internship volunteer opportunities overseas in various English-speaking countries.

Start a muse

A muse is basically a passive online business idea originating from the book *Vagabonding*, and popularized by Tim Ferriss. The purpose of a muse is to make money while you sleep. Passive income to the max!

What is a muse?

A muse is a business that's inexpensive to set up, easy to manage, and generates passive income. Basically, it makes you money while you sleep!

After reading *The 4-Hour Work Week*, we started our own muse. Our personal muse is a group of several Amazon affiliate websites that review different products (also known as niche websites). These websites are very popular in the travel blogging world because they cost very little to set up (although they do require a significant amount of time investment). Although we don't earn enough money to survive solely on our niche websites income, we get a nice $1,500 check every month and plan on growing that business to earn a $10K passive income per month.

Here's where we've learned how to build niche websites: https://www.nichepursuits.com/how-to-build-niche-website/

We are a HUGE fan of niche websites as a passive income source. However, if writing tons of product review articles isn't something that you want to do, here are some steps on how to start a muse:

1. **Start to pay attention to trends**Is everyone eating vegan-friendly bowls this season? Are crocheted bracelets a hit with teenage girls? Find out exactly what people are spending their money on. A great way to discover what's hot, is through Kickstarter, where you can see the types of projects that are getting the most funding. Right now, anything coffee-related is the bees' knees, as are smartphone accessories. Here are some great muse ideas that were successful: https://tim.blog/category/muse-examples/

2. **Test, test, test!**Make sure to run small tests to see if there is a demand for your product or service before launching. You don't want to quit your day job to open a designer indoor cactus store if you are living in Alaska. Kickstarter is a fantastic way to test demand because you'll immediately see if there is demand for your product by how well your project gets funded. If you don't want to run a Kickstarter campaign, put up a simple web page with a product prototype to see if anyone clicks through. You can also run a cheap Facebook campaign for $10 to see if there's any interest. Be sure to research how to target your ads correctly or you may not generate leads properly.

3. **Get started NOW**Too many people wait until they have the perfect idea to launch anything. The result? They never get started. Move forward even if you aren't certain about your idea. You'll certainly pivot along the way as you do more market research during your testing process. You'll start promoting your product or service to your family and friends and, based on the feedback that you get along the way, you can tweak your product/service as you go. A successful business fails, fails, and fails again until they succeed. Never, EVER be afraid to fail. The only regret that you'll have is that you never started.

Here is a great case study of how Noah Kagan built a $4,000-a-month muse in 5 days.

You aren't going to finish and launch your muse idea today, but you should just get your brain juices percolating on what works best for you. Brainstorm, test things, feel things out. Make a list of potential niches you could write about. Explore products that you could sell. This is a chance for you to make money without having to go to a 9-5, so definitely take advantage of it!

24

Day 24: Think outside of the box

Today's challenge: Explore non-traditional methods of travel

Throughout this 30-day challenge, we've explored through many of the typical steps that travelers take to bring their travel dreams to fruition. Today, we're going to switch it up a little bit and think differently.

Here are some non-traditional travel techniques to possibly add to your repertoire:

Student travel grants

If you are a student, there are a world of travel abroad and travel grants available to you. Certain countries offer cultural exchange programs such as Study China and Study India, which are 3-week programs where most of your expenses are covered. There are also longer study abroad programs for a year or more that offer ample opportunities for financial assistance.

Here is a list of student travel grants.

Work on a farm

Love working outdoors? You can explore getting free room, board, and meals by spending some of your traveling time volunteering on a farm. Not only will you get to learn about the food of your chosen region, but you'll also be able to get to exercise altruism! Usually, you are required to stay a minimum of one to two weeks. Of course, you can extend this for as long as you are willing to negotiate. You can explore the farm stay opportunities at WWOOF. Note: there is a small subscription fee.

Apply for The Amazing Race or another travel competition show

Yup, this is totally possible. We applied for The Amazing Race ourselves, although we didn't make it on. It is on Kaila's bucket list to be on a travel TV show, or better yet, HAVE her own travel TV show! We weren't even phased by the million dollars at the end of the competition. We just wanted to travel! On average, during the one-month duration of filming the show, contestants get to travel to 5 continents and 9 countries. While they visit, they complete all types of cultural challenges and invigorating obstacles. It's truly a once-in-a-lifetime experience. All you have to do is find a partner and send in a video to apply!

Crowdfund your travel

We actually used crowdfunding to fund an entire tour in Japan for our former rock band. We just needed around $1,500 extra for the tour, but we ended up earning about $6,000!

We know you might be thinking that sounds crazy. Who is going to give out free money just to send someone else to go on a vacation? Well, you're absolutely correct. Your crowdfunding pitch is going to need a whole lot more meaning than just a simple, "I want to to go to Thailand!"

Crowdfunding is a great option to explore if you are traveling with a meaningful purpose that can resonate with others. Some reasons that would be ideal for crowdfunding include:
1. Writing a book
2. Working with locals to improve the community and bringing money into that region
3. Doing research for a documentary that you want to produce
4. Rebuilding communities damaged by natural disasters

The ideas are endless, but you'll have to spend some time on developing a great intention to travel. Be creative. It will be worth it and may even create a bigger impact rather than just traveling for fun (though there's nothing wrong with that). After all, it's free money for travel, it's worth the time investment!

Here's a list of crowdfunding websites:
- Kickstarter
- Indiegogo
- RocketHub
- GoFundMe
- Patreon
- Crowdrise

Here are some amazing travel Kickstarter campaigns that were funded in the past:

Van Base With Fan Base

One Mile at a Time: The Etihad Residences

The Unseen Africa TV Series

Go Backpacking

Apply for non-student travel grants

Travel grants exist even if you aren't a student, but they require a bit more digging to find. If you are a writer, here's an awesome travel writing scholarship. Here are some other travel grants that you can explore, although they tend to have highly specific requirements.

Enter competitions and giveaways

Ok, we have to admit that we have never won a giveaway in our lives. We haven't entered a ton of them, but we've definitely entered a decent amount. However, our friend Christina won two giveaways in one year, including a trip to Aruba. Perhaps you have more of a lucky streak than we do? Either way, online giveaways from reputable sources often take very little effort to enter so you might as well give them a shot!

Did you come across any interesting ideas during today? Have any unique ideas of your own? Let us know, we would love to hear from you!

25

Day 25: Explore alternative accommodations

Today's challenge: Find an affordable accomodation for your trip

Can you believe that we are 25 days into this crazy journey? You're so close to your travel goals. Don't give up! You got this!

Today we are going to explore some non-traditional accommodations that can switch up your travel game, ten-fold. If you're up for an adventure, keep on reading.

With the current sharing economy, it's so easy to do a housing swap or rent out your place while you are traveling. You may have a free place to stay on your trip or earn enough money to cover the costs of your travels.

Here are some of our favorite alternative accommodation options:

Airbnb

This former startup is now poised to try to take over the travel industry! Not only do they offer affordable hotel alternatives in most locations all around the world, but they are also now offering tours, and even hotel and apartment rentals.

Other options that are similar to Airbnb include HomeAway, VRBO, FlipKey, TripAdvisor Rentals, and Wimdu, to name a few. Some people find that staying in an Airbnb is similar to living like a local; it's basically renting out a room in an apartment, so you get to experience the culture first-hand. Plus, it's a great way to meet other travelers.

The Glamping Hub

We love the Glamping Hub, it's like Airbnb but for glamping! If you aren't familiar with the term glamping, it's basically a more glamorous form of camping, hence: glam + camping = glamping. When glamping, you won't be roughing it as you would camping in a tent, but you will still get the camping type of outdoor experience.

Many of the properties available on the Glamping Hub are actually more like hotels overlooking mountains, or even on the beach. You'll find unusual accommodation like yurts, teepees, tree-houses, and even some tradition cabins (but glammed up, of course!)

Hostels

If you don't mind sharing a room, hostels might be the choice for you. The cheapest hostels often have multiple people sleeping in one room in a bunk set up; think of it as a flashback to summer camp. Hostels have been traditionally frequented by backpackers in their twenties, but these days there are more high-end hostels that offer more amenities, privacy, and even your own rooms. Hostels are also ideal for travelers who are interested in meeting other travelers along the way.

Hostels are often run by travelers, so you're likely to get more personalized attention than you would at a more anonymous hotel. Also, the prices are often negotiable ... all you have to do is ask!

Couch surfing

We don't necessarily mean standing outside with a cardboard sign asking for a couch—there's an actual website called https://www.couchsurfing.com/ that allows you to find a room to stay in. If you find a local on Couchsurfing to stay with, they are actually vetted via the website with their address, credit card number, or mobile phone number, so no worries about being murdered in your sleep. Also, you can also check out the reviews from other couch surfers on the website.

Why couchsurf? Well, number one, it's a totally free place to stay, but one of the other major benefits is that you instantly know someone in a strange, new city. Also, when signing up, you'll fill out a form with your interests, personal information, and hobbies to help you to match up with a host that is similar.

Couchsurfing doesn't just mean that a couch is the only thing available; often, there's a mattress or even an extra room.

Couchsurfing hosts are often hospitable people who are interested in meeting new travelers, so they'll often be a great resource for information while traveling. Also, you'll likely meet a friend in the process. Couchsurfing hosts also accommodate other couch surfers to increase their chances of getting accepted as couch surfers on their own personal travels. Win-win.

Housing swaps

Housing swaps are kind of awesome. Usually, you would use a housing swap service or agency.

How does it work? First, you put up your home on the website and then get connected with another homeowner who would be interested in swapping homes with you for a specific duration of time.

Side note: for a fun movie featuring a housing swap, check out *The Holiday* starring Cameron Diaz, Jack Black, Jude Law, and Kate Winslet. The movie is about two women who exchange houses between Los Angeles and England and find romance along the way. Obviously, romance is not the expected outcome of a home exchange, but sometimes you can get much more out of your travels by staying in someone's home, similar to Airbnb.

You'll definitely experience the city more like a local if that's what you prefer while traveling. Also, you can usually get truly local and unique recommendations from the homeowner about the best hot spots to check out in the vicinity of your housing swap.

Housing swaps are also ideal because you completely save on the cost of hotels during your travels, which is a major expense! The traditional housing swap is the same as in *The Holiday*: Both homeowners arrange to travel to their respective locations at the same time. However, these days, many homestay participants own multiple properties and have more flexibility with their schedules.

Hospitality exchange

Another option is a hospitality exchange where you can arrange to visit as a guest in someone else's home and return the favor by hosting them as a guest in your home at a later date.

Usually, with home exchanges, you'll need to have a lot of flexibility about where you are traveling to. Where you end up going will be determined by the home exchange locations available. If you are dead set on going to a specific location, there are agencies that can broker specific deals such as Home Base Holidays for exchanges to the U.K. or Aussie House Swap for exchanges to Australia, to name a couple.

Also note that home exchanges can be a little more difficult if you live in Kansas, versus a highly-traveled destination like Paris, but with a little more legwork it can definitely be done.

How home exchanges work:

Most websites and organizations have a membership fee—you'll find more opportunities on the websites that do charge a membership fee. In many cases, you can do a search of available listings with or without a membership just to see what's out there.

When doing a home exchange, you want to be flexible with your dates and plan as far in advance as possible. Fill in as many details as you can about your home—this is your selling page! Make sure that the photos are beautifully shot, well lit, and that you list out every amenity that makes your place a selling point.

Also, be sure that you have all the necessary insurance in place before moving forward with the exchange. You want to make sure that if for whatever reason something crazy happens like a house party or a random fire, you are covered. The home exchange hosting company should be able to fill you in on all the paperwork that is required.

Here are some housing swap websites:
- Intervac
- HomeLink USA
- HomeExchange.com
- LoveHomeSwap.com

26

Day 26: How to find cheap flights

Today's challenge: Try out cheap flight hacking methods

So this week, we've explored our top bucket list locations and explored out of the box travel ideas. We're almost there! Let's make it more tangible now and find those affordable flights.

Flights will likely be your largest travel expense, so it really makes sense to spend some time learning the best techniques to find killer flight deals.

My favorite way of finding cheap flights is via Skyscanner. This method involves having a bit of flexibility about the destination that you are traveling to. It's kind of fun, like spinning a Russian roulette wheel; you never know where you're going to land!

Here are the step by step instructions:

1. Go to Skyscanner.net

2. Input your departing city. For the destination city, there's an option called "everywhere." Select that.

3. Choose your dates. When choosing your departing and returning dates, there are several options. Use the "cheapest month" feature, which does require a bit more of a flexible schedule. When you select "cheapest month," it'll show you the cheapest flights available at the moment all over the world. You can also search specific months and specific dates, of course, if you prefer. Try it! It's fun just to see what's available.

To access the "cheapest month" feature, first select "whole month"

Next, click on "cheapest month."

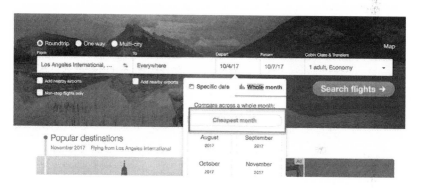

Generally, the cheapest times to fly are January–May and September–December. The most expensive times to fly are June–August and the month of December.

Also, be aware of any major holidays in your destination cities that may affect plane ticket prices and hotel prices. We found an incredible deal on flights to Tokyo, Japan several years ago at $310 a ticket. However, we discovered the hard way that hotels were extremely expensive and difficult to book when visiting Tokyo in April (it was in the heart of cherry blossom season). It's a prime example of slacking on our research skills.

Kayak and *Google Flights* also allow you to search destinations across the entire world to find the cheapest ticket. There's always a deal available to some destination in the world, at any time. If you are flexible about your destination and time frame, you're in it to win it!

Again, be flexible!

You may be able to save money on flights if you are not married to your departure city. For example, we usually fly out of LAX but there are tons of other nearby cities that we can fly out from: Burbank, Riverside, OC, San Diego, etc. If time is not an issue, you can save money by buying a rental car and driving to a cheaper departure city. Also, flying after a major holiday is usually much cheaper than flying prior to that same holiday.

When it comes to picking your arrival city, just focus on getting yourself across the ocean! This means, if we are departing from Los Angeles and want to get to Thailand and we find a super cheap flight somewhere in the vicinity of Thailand, for example in Taiwan, we'll go ahead and purchase the Taiwan ticket. Once we have the international ticket booked, it's much easier to find a cheap flight from Taiwan to Thailand.

Of course, be sure that the extra travel costs and time are worth it for your budgeting.

Budget airlines

Budget airlines are an excellent way to get from point A to point B. However, be very aware that they come with no frills. You'll often have to pay for carry-ons, snacks, and may be penalized for not printing your own tickets and boarding passes. It's not a big deal if you know what are you getting into, just make sure to read all instructions and fine print carefully.

You can save a lot of money by doing your due diligence beforehand. Research the budget airlines available in your country and stalk them! Follow them on social media to keep up to date on the latest flight deals, and join their mailing list to be the first to be informed of any special deals.

There are some killer deals being offered by budget airlines! Earlier this year, WOW air was offering flights from Iceland to the United States for just $99 one way!

There are fewer budget airlines in the United States but there are countless new ones popping up in Europe and Asia.

Also, double-check to see if your preferred budget airline appears on flight search engines such as Orbitz and CheapTickets. For example, Southwest Airlines doesn't appear on these platforms so you would have to search for its flights on Southwest Airlines' website.

If you don't know which budget airlines fly to your destination, just check your destination's airport website to find out which airlines fly in and out of that airport.

You can find a list of budget airlines over at:
https://en.wikipedia.org/wiki/List_of_low-cost_airlines

Airline errors

Error fares are mistakes that are posted by airlines every once in a while, which result in incredibly reduced flight ticket prices. Learn where to watch out for error flights and you can save yourself some serious dough.

One of our favorite sites for this is Airfarewatchdog. Click here for today's most discounted flight prices.

Secret Flying and Scott's Cheap Flights are other excellent sources for getting in the know about these crucial updates. Also, if you use the Skyscanner technique that I mentioned, and look over an entire month, you can sometimes spot error tickets if you see seriously discounted ticket prices.

Book a great deal when you see it

Tickets don't usually get cheaper as your departure date approaches. If you see a great deal, make sure to snag it before it disappears! You'll save the most money when you can book your tickets farther out in advance.

Generally, book domestic flights 1-3 months in advance and international flights 2-8 months in advance. Tuesday, Wednesday, and Saturday tend to be the cheapest days to travel.

If you do want to wait and see if ticket prices drop, certain sites such as *Kayak* and *Google Flights* allow you to set up flight alerts to let you know when the price of your flight fluctuates or changes.

Try many different search engines

When trying to find cheap flights, you'll want to search for a variety of search engines so that you leave no stone unturned. One really cool search engine tool is Momondo because it searches all budget and major airlines and features non-English sites in addition to English language websites.

Student discounts

If you are a student, make sure to check to see if there are any student discounts available on your flights. Search on Google for discount codes or find travel agencies such as *Flight Centre* or *STA Travel* to assist you.

Use points

We covered this topic on Day 19, and it is by far our favorite method of saving on airline tickets. You'll save tons of money and maybe even fly first class if you use points and miles for your travel.

Stalk for deals

Many cheap flights disappear within 24 hours, so you want to be on exclusive flight deals mailing lists to find out about these special deals. Here are some suggested online mailing lists to join: Airfarewatchdog, The Flight Deal, and HolidayPirates.

Search solo flights

Flight search engines will often show more expensive prices when you are searching as a group of travelers, so make sure to just search the price of one traveler at a time. Firstly, you can purchase your tickets individually, and later you can select your seats via the airline's website. When you search for multiple tickets at once, the airline will show you the most expensive ticket options for the flight.

Search other currencies

If the destination that you are traveling to has a weaker currency, try finding that country's version of the airline's website and run a search for the same flight. You might find that when you convert their currency over to USD, the flight can be quite a bit cheaper. Make sure that you use a credit card with no foreign transaction fees or it might eat into any savings that you may have found!

If you take the time to apply these helpful tips, you'll find the stress of booking your flights will be much less. Let's face it, flights can cost you an arm and a leg! Utilizing these methods can really help alleviate that financial stress so you have more room to do what you love while you travel.

27

Day 27: Explore a travel career

Today's challenge: Consider travel as a career choice

When we tell people that we are travel writers, most people are perplexed that the job is even in existence. To be frank, we didn't even discover this career until just a few years ago. Once we were aware that there was a world of people traveling and writing about it for a living, we were completed hooked.

We are both travel writers and travel bloggers, and yes there is a difference. We'll describe exactly what both of those careers are so you can learn more about what options may fit your needs.

Just to be fully transparent, we don't make a full-time income from our travel pursuits; Kaila is also a PR manager and Kiki has multiple social media clients. Most travel professionals do have multiple streams of income to support their endeavors.

Travel writing

If you absolutely love to write, you might want to explore the world of travel writing. Writers of the top travel writing publications are often inundated with press trip offers (seems like a good problem to have). We're not quite at the level of the National Geographic and Travel + Leisure writers.

However, in a year, we scored some nice credits, including writing for Vice, Munchies, Skyscanner, Matador, and many more! Travel writing probably isn't going to make you rich, but the glamorous press trips worth $5K-10K+ might make it well worth your efforts if that's what you're looking for.

Travel blogger

We have several travel blogs in several different niches of travel and receive a nice little passive income check in the low 4 figures every month. We've been working on this blog project part-time for about 2 years, but ultimately, we would like to build these revenue streams up to 5 figures a month.

In the first year, we were able to bring the blog traffic up to 100,000 page views a month, which puts us in the top 5-10% or less of travel bloggers.

There are many media trips that are also offered to top bloggers. We were sent via the India Tourism Board on a 10-day trip to Southern India on a luxury train that costs $7,000 per person. This trip out of pocket would have been worth almost $10,000, including flights!

There are many ways to tackle travel blogging, but we built

our website on the niche site model. You can seriously learn everything you need to know about niche sites by listening to every single podcast and article written by Spencer Haws of *Niche Site Pursuits*. Spencer has since moved on to pursue selling products on Amazon instead of building blogs and affiliate websites, but it's worth listening to all his past work. For the most up to date niche site information, we currently read and listen to everything put out by the *Authority Hacker*.

**We put together a free 5-day email course, teaching you how to get sponsored travel experiences. Check it out and let us know what you think!

Travel influencer

These days, travel brands are often chasing after travel influencers.

Generally, "travel influencers" refers to the owners of social media accounts in the travel space that are popular on Instagram and YouTube. On our trip to India, there were travel influencers (who also had blogs) with 50k/60k followers, which is relatively low in the world of social media.

Travel influencers who are constantly being sent around the world have at least 250k followers. These numbers may sound huge, but don't balk! I've seen plenty of people build up a social media following pretty fast. Instagram has not been our main focus as of yet, but this year we are placing a heavy focus on building our accounts. We've joined a community called *Instagram Decoded* which has a great and totally affordable course to build your following.

Another totally legitimate option is that you could purchase an already-established travel Instagram account with a high number of followers for $1,000-2,000. However, if you do decide to do this, be sure to choose an account that's travel-related.

Tour operator

You should also consider getting a job at a tour company or putting on a local tour for your area to get your feet wet. If you are from a different country or have a little more experience traveling, consider setting up a tour to take travelers to another country!

Kaila's friend, Karen, is a travel writer who specializes in the region of France. Several times a year, she leads a women-only tour through France. She not only gets to share her love for France with a group of tourists, but she also gets paid to travel to her favorite place in the world several times a year. Depending on your entrepreneurial prowess, this can earn anywhere from an extra $1,000 a month to $10,000 a month.

Here's a resource on how to conduct your own tours.

If you decide to fully envelop travel into your life, you'll find loads of opportunities to travel for free. Continually surround yourself in the industry. The signs can't be ignored!

28

Day 28: Reflection

Can you believe that you've made it through 4 weeks? Kudos on powering through and making it to the end. With just a couple of days to go, you are going to be the ultimate travel boss!

Last week, you explored expert hacking techniques for booking flights, explored off the beaten path travel accommodation ideas and all kinds of out of the box ideas. It's always good to explore new ideas and get outside of your comfort zone, especially since traveling usually has you experiencing all kinds of new things! How did you feel about everything? Were there any ideas that you really want to add to your travel toolkit?

One of the most useful steps from Week 4 is viewing your travel dreams through a scope other than your own. By listing out your travel bucket list, you imagined living out your wildest travel dreams, bringing them one step closer to reality. We then discussed different ideas on how certain travelers live a nomadic lifestyle, and other out of the box ways to fund your travel. Not everyone will implement or resonate with all the ideas mentioned, but most will have found some great takeaways!

So often, many of us get stuck with the belief that we can't afford to travel. But, as shown in the last 4 weeks, if we really sit down and explore all the options, travel is very attainable.

It's easy to get stuck in our daily lives, dreaming about travel one day in the far future but never taking any action to make it a reality. Embarking on this challenge forces you to open to your mind to all the possibilities and educate you on how others are actually traveling, often full-time. And no, they aren't wealthy or rich!

With a little bit of diligence, research, and time commitment, you'll find that all of these tools you learned so far will allow you to take actionable steps toward your travel goals. Many of the tools that you have taken away from this challenge will stay with you forever, and you can always revisit the ones that are rusty and give them a quick buff.

You're about to create some serious travel memories that will last you a lifetime. Stories, relationships, feelings, and experiences that will define who you are in the future. It's an exciting time to take a pivot in your lifestyle and start exploring what's outside your own binoculars.

So, once again, here is your weekly reflection sheet. Just take a little bit of time out to scribble down your feelings about this past week and your thoughts on what it means to be finishing the challenge in just a couple of days. Ruminate on your struggles and wins, and especially the lessons you have learned. This process of reflection is always interesting to look back at later on—you'll see just how you've come!

You deserve a round of applause!

30-DAY TRAVEL CHALLENGE

WEEK 4 REFLECTION

WHAT IS YOUR FAVORITE BUCKET LIST TRAVEL AND WHY?

_____

_____

_____

ARE YOU CONSIDERING VAGABONDING? IF SO, NAME THREE ACTIONABLE STEPS YOU NEED TO DO TO MAKE IT HAPPEN.

_____

_____

DESCRIBE ONE ALTERNATIVE WAY OF TRAVELING THAT IS FEASIBLE FOR YOUR LIFESTYLE. WHY WOULD YOU DO IT?

_____

_____

_____

_____

_____

_____

_____

30-DAY TRAVEL CHALLENGE

WEEK 4 REFLECTION

OUT OF THE FOUR TRAVEL CAREERS, WHICH ONE FITS
YOUR LIFESTYLE AND WHY?

_____

_____

_____

WHAT WAS THE BIGGEST TAKEAWAY THAT YOU'VE
GOTTEN THIS WEEK?

_____

_____

_____

_____

_____

_____

_____

_____

_____

_____

29

Day 29: Plan a weekend getaway

Today's challenge: Make your first travel plans!

You're literally 48 hours away from finishing this challenge, the final stretch! It's almost time to celebrate what an incredible win you've just achieved ... but not quite yet! We have just a couple more steps to overcome. You've accomplished so much already—you've explored your own city, done extensive planning for your upcoming trip, and even started a budget for that trip. You've really grown as an aspiring traveler, and we hope that you can see many more travel adventures in your near future.

Your big trip is likely still a couple of months away or more, so it's a great time to plan a weekend trip much sooner. You can do it!

Today's assignment is to step up and plan a weekend getaway or staycation! Don't worry, it's totally possible to plan a weekend getaway on a tight budget unless you have some extra cash to spend. We are going to share some tips on how to plan a weekend vacay that involves visiting places that are in driving distance. It could even involve a staycation in a budget hotel or Airbnb in your same city or driving to a neighboring town.

If you don't want to spend money on a weekend getaway, I've included instructions on how you could even put together a staycation at home, turning off all the cell phones and laptops so you can check out. Just skip this section or scroll to the staycation section for the cheaper alternative

Planning a weekend getaway

Don't want to do too much planning? There's a cool website called Wander to help with your planning a getaway at any budget. Just punch in your dates and your budget and it'll come up with location and accommodation ideas. We put in a 2-night getaway for 2 with a budget of $400, which would only allow getaways that are in driving distance, but we found getaways in Long Beach, Ontario, Palm Springs, and San Diego from $98-$386.

Accommodation

Review Day 25 for alternative accommodation and budget stay ideas!

Here are some additional affordable accommodation ideas:

Are you down to camp or glamp? We worked with the Glamp-ingHub, which had some affordable rental options available. If you are already a camper, it's possible to find camping spots available for as low as $20-30 a night. If you are interested in camping but don't have any camping equipment yet, you can try out a service like Windigo Travel—they rent out all the camping supplies that you might need for your trip.

Don't want to spend the night somewhere else? We recently took a day trip from Los Angeles down to Tijuana, which was a lot of fun. What about going out boating for the day? Boat charters can be fairly inexpensive in the off-season. We have whale watching trips that are super cheap in the Los Angeles area that you can scour Groupon for. Once, we found a whale watching trip on clearance for $15 a person. We ended up seeing a rare superpod of dolphins with over 1,000 of them in total!

Transportation

Road trip

This is probably the most affordable way to take a weekend vacay. It's simple: Just take the car out and drive somewhere! You can just take a weekend getaway at the next city or you can drive somewhere much farther. Pick a spot that's not going to cost you too much gas, around the 500-mile max range. Of course, if you love the road, you can travel as far as you desire.

Flights

Flights are not normally the most cost-effective way to travel on a budget, but if you are planning a last minute weekend getaway, there are usually some really fantastic deals available. Make sure to check Skyscanner and/or review our Day 26 on how to find the cheapest flights.

Food

Pack your food

Picnics are a classic and exciting way to enjoy your weekend getaway. Make sure that you book a place with a kitchen so that you can bring and cook your own food. Eating out cuts into a big portion of travel costs, so if you need to save money on your weekend getaway, buy groceries. It's also fun to build in a trip to a local farmers' market of the city that you are visiting.

Visiting local markets is an excellent way to discover what's growing in your town. Plus, it's always great to support your local vendors. Otherwise, there are plenty of budget restaurants, diners, and holes-in-the-walls that you can find by researching online. Yelp it up!

Activities/tours

Beaches, forests, and historical sites

These points of interest can easily take up your entire weekend and are often extremely low cost or entirely free! State parks are unique to each location and a great part of a weekend getaway.

Self-guided tours

Refer back to Day 5 for self-guided tour ideas.

Community calendars

Check the local community calendars to learn about mostly low-cost activities taking place in your weekend getaway destination. You can even get involved in some charity work—though it may seem like work, there are lots of perks involved when you help your community. You can also learn a whole lot more about your local culture.

Weekend staycation

Not in your budget yet to plan a weekend getaway? We understand that this may be the case since you are saving up for that big trip. Not to worry, you can still plan a weekend staycation to have a fun escape from the regular routine.

Here's how to plan a weekend staycation:

Clean your house

Before you embark on your staycation, you'll want your place to be relatively clean and inviting for your time at home. Take some extra time to tidy the place up before the weekend comes. You don't have to do anything extreme; you just want to make sure that you don't end up doing any cleaning while you are enjoying your break. Kaila is terrible at housekeeping, so when we plan to do a weekend staycation, she'll hire housekeepers to come by before the weekend to get her home in tip-top shape!

Dress up your place

It's time to start exercising your inner interior designer skills. Pick up a beautiful bouquet of flowers for the living room, bedroom, or both! How about taking those special linens and towels out for the bathrooms? Also, go and pick up a fragrant candle for the room. Make sure to change the sheets and fluff up the pillows before the weekend, also. If you are having your housekeeper stop by, let her know to make up your bed, hotel-style!

Abandon your routine

You should abandon your regular routine during your staycation! No catching up on emails or doing any chores. All these things should have been completed beforehand, so be sure you prepared properly.

Room service

If you are planning on a solo staycation, order in from your favorite local restaurant. One of our favorite apps to use for ordering food is *GrubHub*. There's also *Postmates*, *Yelp Delivery*, *UberEats*, and other amazing apps that allows you to get food from your favorite local restaurants delivered straight to your door.

If you are planning to staycation with a loved one or friends, split up the "room service" responsibilities! You can take charge of cooking and serving a meal, and swap with another for another meal. Catch up on Netflix or sleep in while your breakfast is being prepared!

Pick up a souvenir

We like to make staycations extra special by picking up a little memento for the weekend. Maybe this could be matching coffee mugs for the leisurely cups of coffee that you will be enjoying together. Perhaps it's a beautiful wood serving tray for those breakfasts in bed. What about a luxurious set of pajamas to lounge around in all day? Get creative and have fun with the souvenir ideas! You can also buy photo frames where you can put up photos from your staycation in later.

Savor those dinners

Dinners are a great way to connect with friends, family, partners, or even just your own pleasure. That's why they're vital for the staycation experience. Perhaps you'll go dine out at one of your favorite local restaurants or try out a hot spot that you haven't had time to try yet.

What about pulling out the cookbook that has been collecting dust in the corner and trying out one of the recipes that you've been meaning to cook forever? We love really planning out staycation dinners and going all out! Instead of just a regular weeknight entrée, I'll prepare a salad, appetizer, bread, entrée, and dessert. Don't hold back on anything, it's time to indulge!

It's also a great way to incorporate your local farmers' market or gourmet grocery store into the staycation and meal planning process. During the day, I'll take a look at the best ingredients available and will splurge on the ingredients that we wouldn't regularly use on a weekday meal—ingredients like crab, prime rib, etc. Don't be afraid to get the good stuff; it's all a part of the experience.

Break out the fancy wine

Been saving wine for a special occasion? This is the time to break it out! How about pulling out a cocktail recipe and making something fun and seasonal? There's nothing that screams staycation better than kicking back and relaxing with your favorite drink at hand.

Activity inspiration

Go back to Day 6 to review ideas on how to be a local tourist. However, this is a weekend staycation so you are given the complete freedom to lounge around the house and do nothing. You don't need to have a jam-packed weekend schedule for this to be a successful staycation.

Hire a babysitter

It's time to hit up Mom to watch the kids for the weekend! Maybe you can set up a playdate sleep over at someone else's house (and offer to do the same on another night). Otherwise, you can bring your kids along for your staycation, also.

Turn off your phone!

No working allowed during your staycation! Turn off your phone, don't touch that laptop, and delete your work email from your account for this weekend. We don't want anything to distract you from this weekend of relaxation.

Take photos

Whenever we travel, we take tons of photos. Even if you're not comfortable doing it, give it a go! If you're making a delicious dinner, make sure to commemorate it with a photo. Shopping at the farmers' markets and sampling the delicious local eats? Take a selfie or couples photo.

30

Day 30: Create a travel vision board

LAST CHALLENGE: Have so much fun creating your travel vision board

Guess what?

You've made it to the last day of the challenge!

We're so proud of you, and you should be, too. Through ups and downs, highs and lows, good days and bad, you persevered through and made it. It takes a lot of guts and gusto to be able to see it through to the end, and for that reason, we are very proud of you. It really takes commitment and dedication to make it through 30 days of anything.

Today, we are going to work on a vision board, and you'll be able to hang it up somewhere visible in your house to continually remind yourself about your travel goals and aspirations, and also, so you don't let life get the best of you and put your travel dreams on the back-burner.

What is a vision board? It's a poster, board, or sheet of paper showcasing images of what you want your life as a traveler to look like.

Vision boards really do work! They are tangible manifestations of your goals and dreams and can be very powerful. Back when we used to be musicians, Kaila added a Rolling Stone cover to her vision board at the start of the year. Later on, that summer, she was featured in Rolling Stone as one of the female artists to watch that year. She didn't get the magazine cover, but even being mentioned in Rolling Stone with a short write-up was a huge press clipping for her and a great accomplishment.

Here's another anecdote, from Kaila's acquaintance, Sam. Sam is one of Los Angeles' most successful realtors at just 22 years of age. He is hired to speak at real estate and motivation conferences all around the world. He once told Kaila a story about his own vision board experience, which blew her mind. On one of his vision boards was a beautiful model. A few years later he ended up meeting that same model and now they are happily married with two kids...!

Vision boarding practices the principles taught in the very popular book *The Secret*. This book teaches readers about the power of the *Law of Attraction* and how to use the tool of visualization to manifest more of what you want into your life. Olympians frequently use visualization techniques in their training so this is no silly hocus pocus kind of belief!

Visualization works best when you can infuse as much feeling and emotion into it as possible. You have to believe it to see it. Read that over again. When choosing images for your vision board, don't just choose images picturing things that you want, choose images that stir you deep inside and make you viscerally excited!

Here's an example: There's a gorgeous restaurant in Kaila's neighborhood called Fig & Olive. Whenever we enter the restaurant, we get a vast feeling of expansiveness, luxury, and comfort all at the same time. The waiters are generous, attentive, and not at all snobby. The clientele is stylish yet understated and the food is stellar and fresh. You never feel rushed while dining there; long, drawn-out lunch meals are the norm and shared plates are what everyone orders. It's a place that truly sparks an inspirational, emotional response that we can't forget, which is why it has a featured place on Kaila's vision board.

If we come across any mementos like shells or flowers from an amazing trip, we'll also add them to our vision boards along the way. Just one look at one of these travel souvenirs takes us back to the amazing memories that we experienced through our travels.

If you receive any amazing "thank you" cards or birthday cards with messages that fill you with emotion, add them to your vision board. They'll be easily accessed so you can read them frequently for added inspiration.

There are no rules when putting together your vision board. Just add anything to your vision board that makes you excited about your travel life and goals. You can add all the destinations that you ever want to travel to, just the places that you want to go this year, or just the one exotic trip that you are focusing on at the moment. It's totally up to you!

We usually create a new vision board at the start of each year, or start up a new one if we've already traveled to all the destinations featured.

Here's what you need to get started:

Supplies:

- A big sheet of paper, poster, pin board or cork board. Make sure that it's big enough to fit everything you want on it!
- Glue stick, stickers, tape, pins, stapler, etc.—whatever method you want to use to put your vision board together.
- Fun stuff (optional) stickers, glitter, markers—anything fun that you want to use to jazz up your board.
- A stack of magazines or a printer to print images from the web.

Make sure to set aside at least a full hour or two to concentrate on putting your vision board together. Turn your cell phone off and really put your heart and soul into it! You can even turn on some fun music and light a candle, or put on some essential oils to activate your mood. Even better, make an event of it—invite a couple friends over and work on your vision boards together. Friends can help spark other emotional memories and create new ones, too.

We would love to see your completed vision board! Send them to us at kaila@nylonpink.tv

Here's are examples of our vision boards:

Kaila's:

Kiki's:

31

Conclusion

Tomorrow, our travel challenge will be over and you can go back to your regular schedule. We would encourage you to finish up this challenge with purpose, to take the principles of this challenge and incorporate them permanently into your life. We want this to be a new beginning for you, with tons of travel in the horizons and exciting adventures awaiting you.

After today, you can put this book away on the shelf and apply the principles sometime in the far away future. The other choice is that you can continue with the plans that you have made throughout this challenge and bring much more travel into your life. No more dreaming about travel after retirement or when you win the lottery. Take advantage of all the momentum that you've built up throughout this challenge and launch yourself into a world of travel.

Keep saving diligently to your travel saving accounts or accumulating points and miles. Continue to explore your city and take weekend getaways or staycations. Commit to networking with fellow travelers and keep engaging in travel communities to keep your inspiration going.

There will be days where you'll feel discouraged, low, or maybe even just downright tired. Let's face it, starting something completely new out of your ordinary routine can be extremely overwhelming and mind-boggling.

However, the key is to stick to it. Know that there's a bright, beaming, and blinding light of travel heaven waiting for you at the end of the tunnel. Know that all of your discomforts and efforts will soon pay off. Know that every second, minute, and hour that you've worked so diligently at building your travel dreams will certainly bear the fruits of your labor. You WILL succeed if you stick to your guns and keep a positive attitude along the way.

If you ever need a little encouragement with your travel adventures or just in life, feel free to open this book up again. Get excited again; live vicariously through your first 30-Day Travel Challenge, through which we're sure you've built up some fun memories following through the book.

We'll leave you now with one of our favorite anonymous quotes: *"We travel not to escape life, but for life not to escape us."*

Interviews

We interviewed some of the most experienced travelers in the business to fill you in on their tips and tricks about traveling!

INTERVIEW WITH
DAVE'S TRAVEL CORNER

Dave is a well known travel blogger and writer who founded his travel blog back in 1996. We were first introduced to his work via Alexa Meisler William's podcast and later connected with him at a Travel Massive event in Los Angeles. With over 22+ years in the travel game and over 450,000 followers across social media, Dave is truly an expert on all things travel!

Read on for amazing travel tips and insights on how to get started as a new travel blogger.

1. **Coming from the perspective of a travel expert, how do you choose your next travel destination?**

I seek out destinations that offer a diversity of unique and fun experiences, including some adventure and culinary activities (a country with wine regions is also nice). I also identify destinations where I can enjoy a balance between the natural and urban worlds and look for places that offer good value for money.

These days, I am mostly interested in visiting countries I have not yet been to—as I am slowly visiting every country in the world. But often, my next travel destination is chosen for me based on work I do with various travel brands.

2. **What is (are) your favorite travel destination(s), and why?**

My favorite destinations are about experiences—parts of the world that are memorable because of the people I meet and their generosity towards strangers. This is generalized, but I often find that the poorer a country is financially, the more generous the people are to strangers.

I love travel destinations that offer a variety of intriguing foods and festivals—also, very important to me is a destination that combines both inspirational human and natural elements. When I travel I love to spend time in both the urban and natural worlds.

And I can answer this question by a continent or regions...There is nowhere on the planet quite like **Antarctica** with its extreme weather, wildlife (both above and below the sea) and impressive mountains and ice.

Africa—I gravitate towards Sub-Saharan Eastern Africa. The wildlife is prolific in parts of some of the countries. I recommend everyone to do an African safari at least once in their life.

Australia and New Zealand for the diversity of terrain and experiences.

Micronesia—definitely Palau.

Asia—Thailand

Middle East—Jordan, Iran, and Oman.

Europe—hard to choose. The Alps are gorgeous but I've had memorable trips to lesser known countries, including Macedonia and Montenegro. The latter being home of Europe's southernmost fjord.

North America—I'm very partial to my home state of California.

Central America—Costa Rica

South America—definitely Peru. Also Argentina and Brazil.

3. **Wow, your blog has been online since 1996! What do you think has allowed your blog to thrive as many others fall**

by the wayside?

My personal passion for travel, but more importantly, my ability to stick with projects and continue to develop the site. And my willingness to live cheaply, especially in the early days when my site was a hobby and not making any money.

Also being among the early travel sites has certainly helped with visibility—and the more time one puts into this, the more connections one makes as far as networking. And networking over the years has led to more exposure for my site, and to also directly working with a number of travel brands.

Adding a customized and fairly easy to use author content back-end management system which integrates into WordPress was a huge step forward for my blog. Quite a few blogs will accept guest posts but do not have a system for handling larger volumes of content. Before, I was accepting contributions from writers via email—today, one creates an account and uploads content, including photos. I am notified and then I can edit and schedule the post for publication. It is so much more streamlined than in the early days.

This has expanded the number of contributors to my blog, thus helping to grow the overall content of my site. When brands or destinations offer press trips, it has given me a large pool of writers to choose from when I am unable to attend a trip or event.

Incidentally, my research confirms the huge turnover in travel blogs. For example, I maintain a list of over 6,000 in English www.xxx.xxx travel blogs on my site—I began this list around 2006 (has been as high as nearly 10,000). I update this once a year and each time I do I remove 800-1200 links because they are no longer active.

4. How have you seen the blogging landscape change throughout those years?

Huge changes have occurred in the digital space in some 20+ years since I began my site—the three biggest being availability and access of content, the ease of creating content, and the advent of social media.

When I began my site, the online world was more a domain for techies i.e., bulletin boards, and BBS systems were still popular where users would dial in with a slow modem and connect to communities, which were often gaming related, where the communities were created around a text-based interface rather than a visual interface.

Along with slow Internet, content creation platforms were extremely cumbersome and difficult to use with plenty of bugs. My first editing software for my travel site was a crappy product put out by Microsoft called Front Page.

Now we have WordPress and other easy to use blogging

platforms. But back then, these did not exist.

Blogging wasn't even a 'thing' in the late 1990s—there wasn't a specific software platform for blogging and the term 'blogger' had not yet been mentioned. If you wrote about your personal travels in the early days, it was a basic online journal.

5. How would you recommend a new blogger to get started?

If you want to make money from blogging and related activities, you must approach your work from the perspective of running a business rather than running a hobby travel website. At the same time, let your personality and passion for travel show through as much as possible in your blogging.

Regardless of your background, if you enjoy writing, follow your passion but become a better writer in the process. Editing is a huge part of the writing process that many travel bloggers neglect, and it may have hurt the reputation of the industry as a whole—especially in its infancy a decade ago (in part because many travel bloggers do not have a background in journalism).

I learned this from working on my wine website, often editing a post 10 to 20+ times, revisiting over a period of a week or more, especially in the mornings when I am fresh. Tighten your sentence structure—using less words to say the same thing is perfectly fine.

Have another income source to begin with that allows you to invest in building and growing your travel blog and social media presence. Do not get stuck in doing menial things. There are resources you can utilize to outsource work such as SEO building, social media management, and growth and content creation. There are plenty of people willing to do these tasks at reasonable prices (I have used a variety of sites over the years). Find the the right person and build up trust around a working relationship.

I cannot stress the importance of networking enough—in person rather then just networking online. Go to travel events such as Travel Massive or meetup events focusing on travel. Attend travel blogger related events—TBEX is probably the largest, but there are also a number of more regional travel blogger events and various travel trade shows that a quick search will uncover.

It's so easy to be just another travel blog in a sea of travel blogs, so developing personal relationships with the right people is very important, including other travel bloggers who are more established than you, PR people, and various brands working in the travel space.

Sometimes, I am asked how many followers should I have before I begin approaching brands. Brands may want 10,000 or many more than that, but sometimes less if you focus on a very niche topic and have good interaction among your followers. There is no right answer here, other than the more real followers you have, the more power you will carry when dealing with brands that want to work with you, and often the greater the payoff.

Become an expert in a specific region and create good content around that, and then figure out a way to monetize that content. For example, I have become a winery expert in the Napa Valley and have the content online to prove it—so I began offering concierge and tour services—and my wine content has become a platform from which I acquire new customers.

6. **What are your plans for Dave's Travel Corner in 2019?**

To continue to add content to the site and to expand my current list of contributors (around 600 right now). To spend more time on SEO. To look again at select affiliate platforms, including Mediavine. And I'm thinking of reintroducing what used to be our annual travel writing contest—a chance for anyone who enjoys travel and writing about travel to submit for the chance to win various prizes.

And personally, I will be visiting Haiti, my last county in the Caribbean to explore. I will also visit Mongolia later in the year.

Related to my other life, which involves visiting, tasting, and writing about every single Napa Valley-based winery, producer or tasting room (997 visits and reviews completed to date—I often travel outside of Napa to gather content, I will be doing a Napa Valley-focused trip to Europe this May, visiting numerous wineries and spaces in several countries with strong ties to the Napa Valley. I'm sure this will also result in additional content on Dave's Travel Corner.

Brands reach out throughout the year, so I never know in which direction my work travels will take me.

Related links as mentioned above:

997 Napa Valley based wineries, producers or tasting rooms visited to date
Travel Blog directory
Finding virtual assistants

INTERVIEW WITH
LOIS ALTER MARK

Lois Alter Mark is a writer that we absolutely look up to! She's an award winning blogger at <u>Midlife at the Oasis</u>. She also writes for Forbes, USA Today, has won multiple BlogHer awards, and even went on a trip to Australia with Oprah. She is living out her bucket list dreams after 50, which has helped inspire avid travelers from all over the world.

1. **How did you get into travel writing?**

I've been a writer forever, and I decided to try travel writing once our kids were grown and out on their own. I started by writing on my blog about luxury hotels and places my family or my husband and I visited, then started pitching stories. I'm now a regular contributor to USA Today, 10Best, and Forbes, and also write for a few AAA magazines.

2. **What advice would you give to someone who thinks they can't afford to travel?**

I met a woman at the Churchill Northern Studies Centre in Canada, who was volunteering there, getting to see the Northern Lights and polar bears and Beluga whales—and getting room and board—in return for working in the kitchen. She had spent a year traveling around the world for almost nothing by doing volunteer work like this. I thought it was brilliant because she got to experience so many great things she would never have been able to afford otherwise.

3. **We love that you are celebrating your midlife, that's a total girl power move! What advice would you give to those trying to discover what makes them happy?**

Just start! Step out of your comfort zone and try new things. I didn't start travel writing until I was in my 50s and certainly never anticipated making a career out of it. I think it's important to be open. You never know where life will take you.

4. **You mentioned that you had a hard time falling asleep on flights. What are your favorite ways to pass the time on long haul flights?**

I read and watch a lot of movies! Sometimes I clean out the photos on my phone and my laptop. I so admire people who can fall asleep on a plane. That is truly a gift, and one that I just don't have.

5. **What was it like traveling with Oprah?**

Amazing and totally surreal.

I was chosen as an Ultimate Viewer because of my blog, which was inspired by her, and 300 of us went to Australia with her on the trip of a lifetime. I got to hug a koala, snorkel in the Great Barrier Reef, enjoy a private beach party on the Whitsundays hosted by Chef Curtis Stone, and actually spend time talking to Oprah and Gayle. I learned a huge lesson on this trip when my friend said, "It doesn't get better than this," and another guest told her, "You never say that. You ask, 'How does it get better than this?' and let the Universe show you."

That was a real Oprah "aha" moment.

6. **What are your favorite destinations?**

Oh, I have so many! There's something I love about every place I visit, but I especially love Africa, Iceland, Ireland, Norway, Thailand (where my family spent four days volunteering at the Elephant Nature Park, and learned NEVER to take an elephant ride or support circuses or shows that feature performing elephants) ... and I will go anywhere on a Viking ocean cruise.

7. **What are you working on and where are you traveling to this year?**

I just got back from Las Vegas, Orlando, and Phoenix, and am hoping to get to Newfoundland, Hay-on-Wye, and, oh, did I tell you how much I love Viking ocean cruises?

INTERVIEW WITH
JACKI UENG

Jacki is our girl and founder of the Bohemian Vagabond blog. We can't wait to go on a trip with her! A fellow Angeleno, she has found financial freedom via real estate investing, and has gotten us passionate about it, too! She's a solo female traveler and talented writer. In our interview, she shares with us how she got started in the world of real estate.

1. **We love that you are able to fund your travels via real estate investing. When did you first start investing in real estate?**

I bought my first house at the age of 25 years old in 2010. I had $15,000 saved and so I used FHA financing to put 3.5% down on a $275,000 house in San Bernardino County. The timing was also perfect as we were in the midst of the recession (prices were incredibly low) and there were also 2 tax credits available for first time home buyers:

1) A Federal Credit from President Obama at $8,000, and 2) a State Credit from California of $10,000. The house was essentially free for me.

The property is now worth about $475,000. Once I had a taste of it, I became addicted. As soon as I saved more money, I started looking into 2-4 units and bought a 3-unit in 2012. I sold that 1.5 years later and took the earnings and exchanged it into a 4-unit building. It was a riskier buy as 3 of the units were vacant, but that also meant that I was able to fix it up and rent them out at market rent, which also meant that the value of my property went up immediately after.

My next savings went to a 2nd home near Palm Springs with 15% down. My goal is to purchase and/or exchange 1 property (or unit) a year. I have some catching up to do this year!

2. **A common objection to investing in real estate is "I can't afford it, I'm just trying to get by." How would you recommend a new investor to get started?**

My example above should show that you don't need a lot of savings to get started. There are 3 main options:

a. Purchase your first home with a little down payment (as little as 3.5%), but keep in mind that this is riskier as you'll have a 96.5% loan, so if the property value goes down you could easily be under water on a property you live in. But know that real estate (most of the time) is cyclical and will go back up. It also depends on where you live. Certain real estate markets are more stable than others (i.e., Los Angeles vs. Detroit)

b. A better option (in my opinion), is to use the little savings you have to buy a smaller investment property. If you don't have enough savings to buy your "dream home" or even a "practical home" in the city of LA (that would cost at least $500,000), then buy an investment property at $250,000 in an area you would likely not live in. This way, you can start growing your money instead of having it sit in a bank.

c. Even if you have NO savings but want to get into the real estate game, start studying everything there is about real estate and become a "syndicator." This means you will be dedicating your time to learning. Then you can identify an investment and pull in investors while taking in a percentage as a service fee, as well as position yourself in there to get a cut if/when you resell it.

If you are not ready to invest in real estate, put that money in a high interest savings bank account, such as CIBC (a Canadian bank that is FIDC insured, among many others you can find online), where I am getting 2.4% return and I can pull the money out at any time. The worst thing you can do is to have your money sit in your bank at 0.02% return or to invest in stocks that you don't understand.

3. **What is one of your most memorable solo travel experiences?**

My first solo trip to India (3 weeks) at the age of 23 was the most memorable because it was my very first one and it, overall, went pretty smoothly. That was the official start of my travel blog as well, which began casually for friends and family to live vicariously through my daily adventures. Back then (2008), there weren't as many travel blogs and so the blogging community was much smaller and intimate. I'm still connected to several bloggers I met back then.

4. What are your favorite destinations to travel to?

Lebanon, India, Myanmar (Burma), Taiwan, Italy, Greece (and... Israel, Morocco)

5. What are your plans for 2019 and where are you off to next?

I just came back from a trip to UAE (Dubai & Abu Dhabi), Oman, and 2 weeks in India. I am off to explore a new resort in Cabo San Lucas with a PR company I have collaborated with a few times to produce blog posts, photography, and awareness. Heading back to India the end of April for a friend's wedding in Mumbai & Pune. Really hope I finally make it to Japan this year. I'm also heading to another friend's wedding in Macedonia in September (Sicily during that trip and hopefully a few more Eastern European countries I haven't been to yet).

6. **Where can readers find you?**

BohemianVagabond.com, and Instagram, Facebook, Pinterest @bohemianVagabond

INTERVIEW WITH
RICHARD KERR
AWARD TRAVEL 101®

We've been members of Richard Kerr's awesome Award Travel 101® Facebook group for a while now, which is recommended in this book. He's not only a lieutenant in the Navy aviation community, he is also a senior contributor to The Points Guy blog. Richard is a travel hacking master and in our interview below he shares with us his best tips and tricks on how to make the most out of his Facebook group.

1. **How did you start the Award Travel 101® Facebook group?**

I got really good at researching PowerPoints and miles while in Japan and people started asking how I was doing it. I started an online class in Japan where I would wake up early before work and teach people in The States. When my first class was done I wanted a place for us to hang out, so I started the Facebook group back in near to the end of 2013. That's how the group started, mostly with alumni students at first, but more and more people kept joining and it just grew from there.

2. **What advice would you give to a new member of your Facebook group Award Travel 101® to make the most of it?**

So for somebody just joining, Facebook groups are interesting because posts come and go rather quickly, so you kind of have to first learn how to use the group you joined. Every group pretty much has its own guidelines and rules. I would recommend starting with reading the master thread. We have beginner guides, weekly threads that are predictable, and Q&As Thursday nights.

Just take the time to explore and learn as much about the group as possible.

3. **Great, that's awesome advice! So what advice do you have for someone just getting started in travel hacking?**

That's about a 3,000-word answer! The first thing you need to do is set expectations. If this was easy then everybody would do it, but it's not something that you can pick up in 5 minutes. You have got to be willing to invest the time. So the first step is you need to prepare yourself. Know that if you are willing to put in the time to do it, there are great rewards in it, but it's not going to happen overnight.

The second thing that people need to do is make sure your personal finances are in order, that your credit score is high enough that you are going to be able to be approved for credit cards, and that you can spend on the credit cards responsibly. After that, it's time to set a goal. If you try to learn everything about award travel without a goal in mind, you're likely to get lost and it's going to become overwhelming.

So the best thing you could do is, for example: If you want to go to Paris, what airlines fly to Paris? How do those airline rewards programs work and what hotels would you like to stay at in Paris? How do those hotel rewards programs work? Focus on that one single goal and keep your blinders on, because it's easy to get distracted.

4. **I love the goal-oriented perspective. I am really good at earning points but I'm really bad at finding awards flights that are available. Can you tell us more about the points consultant service that you have?**

There are plenty of services out there that anybody can hire. It's extremely complicated sometimes to book award travel, especially if you have to travel to set places on fixed dates.

I don't recommend that you hire a service, rather that you learn how to book award flights on your own, but I understand completely the limitations some may have, especially with time restrictions. Sometimes it makes sense to pay somebody $100 to book you a $5,000 flight.

5. **Yes, it's a good deal! What is one of the most memorable trips that you have achieved through points and travel hacking?**

One of the most memorable trips was back in 2014. I was looking on the Chase awards website and a first class pops up for Etihad First Class—a fare of $900 from Tokyo to Abu Dhabi, and 3 days later from Abu Dhabi to Maldives. I would spend 5 days in the Maldives and then from the Maldives, head back to Abu Dhabi, and from Abu Dhabi back to Tokyo. The total was $900 for a first class international flight round trip—this is a flight that is $10,000 per flight. It was a mistake fare.

So I book the flight for my wife and I. The confirmation says first class, however the information on the Etihad website said business class. Now, $900 for business class is a heck of a deal, but the travel hacker in me had me call Chase and let them know about the discrepancy.

After a couple of days, I received an email of a receipt

from my Chase corporate card that they will be paying the fare difference in order for us to fly in first class. We flew the full $10,000 fare to the beach first class on Etihad Airlines, and my son was a baby at the time. The flight even included a flying nanny that took care of my son during the flight. There was a full chauffeur to and from the airport and we spent three days in Dubai at Park Hyatt Dubai.

I got a haircut and a shave at the first class lounge. They drove us in a luxury car out to the plane. We spent five days in Maldives before flying back home. Etihad also had a triple miles promo going on at the time. So we even got like 200,000 miles from the flight, which got me American Airlines flights for the next two years for free. So it was like the perfect combination of things working out.

6. **Wow, those are serious hacking goals to aspire to! What are some of your favorite airlines and why?**

Well, if I am flying domestically, Delta is my favorite domestic airline. Their onboard products, modernizations, and their fleet compared to anybody else flying is just miles ahead. Also, I'm in Atlanta, so I can fly anywhere non-stop. Internationally, it's really hard for any of the US carriers to compete with Emirates, Etihad, and any of the Asian airlines; they are just so much better, from the quality of the hard product to the the seats and the layout of the cabin, all the way to catering and the services that they offer.

So any of these Asian airlines are my favorites, including Korean Airline, Japan Airlines, ANA, Cathay Pacific, followed shortly there by Etihad and Emirates. If you are going to fly internationally, do yourself a favor and you take a flight from one of these—you're going to be very happy.

7. **So, what are some of your favorite places to visit if you could even narrow it down?**

Vietnam is my favorite country. I had odd expectations going there and especially as a member of the US Armed Forces, because at the time 35 years ago, we were trying to annihilate each other. So I didn't know what to expect and all I saw was an incredibly friendly place, full of people who were just as curious about me as I was about them. It's also very affordable and I just love everything about it.

I also love Scandinavia, and Denmark is my favorite European country. I recommend riding the train or renting a car and driving across Denmark.

I am not a beach guy but the smaller islands in Hawaii are great and they are becoming more and more affordable.

The only one place that I have been that I am not going to go back again is Cambodia.

8. **Where is the best place for everyone to find you, and are you working on anything exciting this year?**

Oh yes, we have got a lot going on with the Award Travel 101 and Award Wallet blog. My podcast is launching this year in just two weeks at the beginning of March; the Award Travel 101 podcast. We've got some really great episodes lining up to launch our series—I am really excited about that.

The Award Wallet blog is getting an entire visual makeover right now. It's going to include even stronger writers and a lot more content, and I also will be writing a lot over there. And we have some pretty unique partnerships with some national brands coming up here this year for Award Travel 101. So a lot going on in our little neck of the woods.

We had some of the best stories from over the years and I have gotten in contact with the Facebook group members and they are going to be my first guests to talk about some of the things they have done. And we've got a mileage broker guy who makes a full-time income mileage brokering. I am excited about it!

INTERVIEW WITH
BETH SANTOS
FOUNDER OF WANDERFUL

Beth Santos is a beast, and we love that she is all about women's empowerment. She is an inspiration for all female entrepreneurs and is dedicated to changing the way the travel industry operates, especially in relation to the recognition of women in the industry. She first started Wanderful as a travel blog and built it to where it is now: An organization of over 40,000 women, which encompasses 30 cities worldwide, and includes a conference and now a home-sharing network. In this interview she drops some serious knowledge on how she accomplished it all.

1. **For those who aren't familiar with Wanderful, could you tell us more about the organization?**

Wanderful is an international community of women who love to travel. And basically, our goal is to help empower and support women, who either already are or are interested in traveling abroad. We do that in a few ways and we have 40,000 women in our network now and they gather for events in 46 global chapters.

So women can use us to meet other women around the world when they are on the road, or also just find somebody else who loves to travel in their own home city. We also have an online community right now on Facebook, as well as on our website. And you can use that for tips and ideas to get feedback on places to go, or things to do or even just other questions related to your experience abroad.

We run a number of global events and trips, so we do a couple of small trips for women. This year we are going to Morocco, India, and Cuba, and then we also run a retreat called Wonder Fest and a conference, which is more of a professional conference called the Women in Travel Summit. And then, finally, because we clearly aren't doing enough already, this year we are launching an international home sharing network for women.

So now, not only can women be helpful to each other in terms of offering advice and ideas and sisterhood, but they could actually stay with each other wherever they are around the world, and find somebody that they can trust to share their experience with. So, yes, that's what we do!

2. **That's pretty amazing because safety is definitely an issue, especially with solo female travelers becoming more of a trend. What are the special requirements to join the homesharing network?**

So the homesharing network is identity verified. There is a three-step identity verification process that we are bringing in. One of those steps is a video verification. So we will spend a couple of minutes, on video, just to make sure that you are the person that you say you are, that you match your profile picture.

I think it adds just a little level of comfort for everyone participating, both on the host's as well as on the travelers' side. We also have a couple of interesting features that we are introducing a little bit later down the line, including like video walkthroughs of your home, so you can see that it wasn't a stock photo that somebody uploaded, that this is actually her house.

Then, of course things like reviews, community flagging, and that sort of thing. So it makes it a little bit more trustworthy. It's definitely by and for women in the community, although we are an inclusive community so we really welcome everyone. But I think that we've definitely found that there are women who are looking for an alternative that's more empowering to women.

So, by adding that in, while also really integrating that with our events and our chapter activities, it even adds a couple things that bring in additional income for the host, including things like, you know, the ability to offer breakfast or do an airport pickup. And so now, we are really creating these rich connections between women that are happening right on the ground. And not just traveling from Boston to San Francisco, but traveling to completely new places where the culture is different and you are really hoping for somebody who can help you on the ground.

3. That's amazing! You've really thought about everything that the other networks don't offer.

You know, we try, and I think we are definitely learning to, but because we have really grown as a community as our own over the last few years, I think it has given us a lot of really good insights into what women are looking for. And sometimes it doesn't have anything to do with safety; sometimes it's just about wanting to be able to support another woman, or understanding that a woman's ability to earn income directly affects the economic health of her town.

And I think women are tuned into that, and so we've really done a lot of outreach to our community to figure out what people are looking for. But also, there is a fear there, and we have seen that it's real. We have just published a survey a couple of weeks ago, and we found that, I think it was like, 30% of women at one point in their lives considered traveling solo but then opted out.

And then when you ask them why, usually it has something to do with concerns about "my own safety," and "my family's concerned about my safety." Or even just not wanting to feel lonely and so there is certainly a gap here that we are finding, where a lot of women really are interested in traveling by themselves. But then there is something holding them back, and so we're hoping that by having that one person, and having that friend who is there who can welcome her into her home, it just closes that gap a little bit.

4. **I love that, that's very thoughtful. So the Women in Travel Summit is a conference for women travelers. What challenges did you have putting together the first conference?**

Oh my gosh, what challenges didn't we have? It was a completely new experience for us. I think when we first decided to host the conference it was literally because our whole foundation came from our blog, and I was doing a lot of my own travel. And starting in 2009, I started writing about my own experience. At that time, blogging was only really starting to become a thing, and even then it was kind of like live journaling; it wasn't really journalism. I think about 2013 we started to see a lot of people were actually taking blogging very seriously. And we thought we should really create something that's bringing people together under this context.

So the people who are building these blogs really want to learn how to do it well. This was even before any of this became a business. No one was making money off of it quite yet. But we thought, "Here's a really neat opportunity to really explore the growth of blogging as an industry."

Now it's much more industry focused. But I will tell you, we didn't know anything about planning a conference. I mean, I really look back and people ask us, "Had you planned conferences before?" or "Had you come from an event planning background?" Really, the only thing I had planned prior to the conference was my wedding for 180 people. So I thought, "How hard could planning a conference be?"

We thought we could plan the whole thing in four months. We literally started in October and had the event in March. We thought that was plenty of time, but it turns out that it's not.

Also, we didn't realize that you actually should stop ticket sales at a certain point. We didn't realize the concept of selling out and we were expecting about 100 people. In fact, we told the hotel we would have 100 or maybe max 150. And I remember we actually sold 183 tickets. At that moment, we realized that we had to stop; the hotel couldn't accommodate any more people.

There were so many lessons along the way. But I think it actually was fun that we didn't have any conference experience, because it sort of allowed us to question the norms of what a conference is.

We just planned it how we thought it should go, and we definitely made mistakes along the way. And even now we are learning things. But overall, the lack of experience gave us a lot of freedom to be creative.

5. **What advice would you give to young entrepreneurs starting new projects?**

There is a level of confidence I think that you have to have as an entrepreneur. You not only have to be 1,000% confident that this business is going to work, but you also have to convince pretty much everybody else.

And the beginning of starting a business is that. I think the most underestimated skills, in my opinion, that exist are sales and storytelling. There is so much value in being able to communicate effectively about your project and how it benefits others. You'll also have to sell your vision to your team and your advisors.

You have to remember that sometimes you are going to feel like it's not going to work. And you have to have the self-awareness to know when those moments are happening, and also know that they will pass and to just keep fighting.

Also, there is no shame in having a side hustle. I don't think that you necessarily need to start a business, and be starving and only eating ramen. I don't think that's the right way to live, either. There isn't any shame in waiting tables, or doing whatever you have to do to give yourself the flexibility to pursue what you are trying to build.

My number one recommendation for an entrepreneur is to take a sales class. It is just such a useful skill to have to really be able to show people your perspective and to uncover what their needs are at the same time.

6. **For those who think they can't afford to travel or don't have the time to travel, what would you tell them?**

I actually workshop a question often in some of my events. And the question is this: "Is travel a responsibility or a privilege?" It's a really interesting conversation and people have asked me, "What's the right answer?" And of course, there is no right answer.

But really, I think what happens when we do that workshop is people start to define "what is travel?" Because, whether or not travel is a privilege or a right depends on what we are talking about.

So to start, can you travel in your own country? Yes! Can you travel within your own state? Yes! Then you can ask if you can travel within your own neighborhood? This is when people start thinking differently. How close can you go from where you live and still be traveling, and what is travel exactly? Also, what are the different representations of travel? Sometimes travel is going on vacation and other times you can travel from right inside your own home.

Sometimes, travel is business-related. Other times, travel can happen when you read a book—you travel with your mind to a different place. So I think the first thing you have to do is really figure out what you are talking about when you say the word "travel."

For me, travel is about opening up your mindset and being willing to make yourself uncomfortable and trying something new. And those are the three key things, and because of that, travel exists on a spectrum. It's the reason why I am really excited about our homesharing network. It's because I believe that you can travel without even leaving your home. Because it's about bringing other people in and exposing yourself to their lifestyles, and opening yourself to their culture. It's a difficult question because I do think that travel is a huge privilege if you are considering traveling in the traditional way, like going to Disney World or traveling outside of your country.

But I also think that there is a lot of travel shaming taking place, that maybe if you don't go far enough or if you don't visit enough countries then you are not actually a traveler. I don't think that's true, and so we really need to examine what it means to travel, and what are the lessons that we learned from travel. We should actually challenge ourselves to see how we can get outside of our comfort zone near our own home, because all of us have those places.

So it's a very long answer for a very short question, but I think it's something that we need to be more purposeful about.

7. **I love it, it's definitely a perspective that most people wouldn't have. What are some plans you have with Wanderful this year?**

At the Women in Travel Summit this year in Portland, we

are launching the Bessie award, which we are really excited about. It is our first ever award ceremony to really honor the voices of women in travel. We have nine categories that influencers are nominated for, as well as brands.

We are going to feature an awesome award experience, with an actual physical award being handed out. It's going to be a night of celebrating all of the accomplishments that women have brought into the travel industry in this past year.

Also, we just announced a second Women in Travel Summit, one that we will be doing every year in Europe.

Our first WITS in Europe is happening in Riga, Latvia, in November. We are really pumped, Riga is a beautiful city. We are also really hoping to open ourselves in to Europe and to North Africa, Asia, and the Middle East, and expand some of those areas because, although our North America event has amazing, we've also found that there are so many other influencers out in the world that aren't able to make it into the US as easily. We want to be able to reach them, too.

So those are some of the big things that are happening over here. It's an exciting time!

8. **Where can everyone find you?**

Our website is www.sheiswanderful.com and all of our

social media handle follow that same pattern, on Twitter, Facebook, Pinterest, Instagram, all @sheiswanderful. And that's wonderful with an "a," not with an "o," of course.

And then, my own self, I have my own website that's bethsantos.com, and I am on Twitter at @MaximumBeth.

INTERVIEW WITH
VALERIE JOY WILSON

Valerie Joy Wilson is the highly accomplished founder of the blog Trusted Travel Girl and believes in travel that fully immerses you into another culture. She wears many hats as a solo-female traveler, journalist, host, photographer, entrepreneur, and more. Traveling is her lifestyle and we can't wait to see her hosting her own travel series in the future!

1. **We love that your blog is all about adventure and girl power. What tips would you have for a first time solo traveler?**

First time solo travelers should know that the scariest part of their trip is just booking the ticket. Start small, try another country where English is widely spoken. Places like

Norway, UK, Australia. Those are good baby-steps.

2. **Were there any destinations that you didn't feel safe traveling solo?**

Only in Brazil. I felt unsafe the entire time, and it wasn't an enjoyable feeling. I didn't let it keep me from doing anything, I went out in Lapa (a dangerous part of Rio) to go samba dancing, but it still was very nerve-racking.

3. **Are there any destinations that you recommend for brand new solo travelers?**

SE Asia is great because there's always a ton of other solo travelers. It makes it easy to meet other travelers so you feel less alone.

4. **We love that you champion traveling like a local, how would you recommend a traveler best immerse themselves in a new destination?**

Sit at the bar of your restaurant instead of a table. People at bars are generally more chatty, or you can talk to your bartender. Find out where they hang out and where other locals go. they will give you way better information than a hotel concierge.Also, local experiences are now offered on platforms like Lokal Travel are great ways to connect you with authentic experiences curated by locals.

5. **What are your favorite destinations to travel to?**

I loved Myanmar, Cuba I have been to multiple times, Norway was incredible!

6. **What are your plans for 2019 and where are you off to next?**

I'm in the middle of pitching a travel show, so I've been quite grounded here in LA for the last two weeks and I'm not used to it. I'm speaking at the Philly Travel and Adventure Show, then off to Europe.

7. **Where can readers find you?**

TrustedTravelGirl.com

instagram: @trustedtravelgirl

facebook.com/trustedtravelgirl

INTERVIEW WITH
ALEX CHACON

Alex is truly an inspirational dude, with an awesome attitude towards adventure and living your best life. Known as one of the top motorcycle travel YouTubers in the world, he left his role as a medical student to explore his passion for travel and sharing his adventures with his loyal followers. He has traveled to over 60 countries and is most famous for traveling the world via motorcycle for 7 years.

We had the honor of tapping into his brain for a bit of knowledge that will truly inspire you to get out and see the world!

1. **What was the catalyst that inspired you to travel the world?**

When I was a little kid in school I would look at a globe and wonder what the world looked like. One day, I spun the globe and put my finger randomly on it until it stopped. It landed on Peru. At that moment, I promised myself I would visit Peru as soon as possible. This seed and idea grew over the next 15 years, until finally I finished college and decided I was going to be one of the people that actually kept their promise to travel the world after college. And this promise from 15 years ago was the seed to the idea, and finishing college was the catalyst to keep that promise to myself.

222

2. **Why did you choose to ride a motorcycle as your main form of transportation?**

When I first set off to travel around the world at 23 years old, money was a big issue. Luckily, I had no debt from college thanks to scholarships I acquired, but I did sell everything I had in order to set off around the world, and a major determining factor as to how long I could travel for was money. I first wanted to visit Machu Picchu in Peru, and as I calculated the costs of flights and transportation, I saw other tourist sites I wanted to visit nearby like Rainbow Mountain. Then, I figured if I'm already there I might as well go to Bolivia and its Uyuni salt flat. Then, said, "Well, Brazil's not too far away from there either," and the snowball effect continued.

I quickly realized that getting to all these places would be costly, and was unfamiliar with how traveling really worked. So I said, "Well, for the same cost of flights and transportation, I can just drive there," and so I did. I then realized that I was able to go at my own pace, visit places no tourist usually visits, and I was able to create an incredible adventure traveling by land, across the world that most people will never understand, nor have the opportunity to do. From then, I fell in love with becoming a terrestrial astronaut.

3. **How do you find the most affordable accommodation on your travels?**

When I travel, I usually stay at hostels and use the various internet search engines for accommodation, to find cheap affordable places to stay. When I travel by motorcycle, I usually camp out in beautiful wilderness areas. When I feel adventurous I do couchsurfing, and even just meet people on the road that love my story and what I'm doing, and they invite me into their homes.

4. **Where are the best places to travel on a budget?**

Any place can really be traveled to on a budget if you know what you're doing and are creative enough and willing to sacrifice some comforts. However, for the average traveler, the places where I've found your money goes furthest is Latin America and Southeast Asia.

5. **What is the first thing you plan when budgeting for a trip?**

First thing I look at when planning a trip is over all costs and the time frame—how much time I have to travel, costs of getting and surviving there, costs of tours, stay, and food. Then, I calculate if I have enough time there to make it worth it, meaning would I rather spend $2,000 USD for 1 week in Europe or $3,000 USD for 4 weeks in South America? That's why most trips of mine are 1-4 months, as it's more cost effective to go non-stop and see as much as you can before coming back home. Most times, it's cheaper to live on the road than to come home, for me.

6. **Have you faced any difficult situations when it comes to budgeting for adventure travel? How did you overcome them?**

When I first started traveling at age 23 my biggest obstacle was money, but I didn't let that stop me. I was willing to sacrifice everything to make it happen. That's why I took a motorcycle around the world. My first major trip was riding from Alaska to Argentina in 500 days.

I only had budget for 4-6 months at the beginning, but my determination was more powerful than anything. I survived by only spending money on gas, spare parts, and hostels. I ate canned beans, slept in parking lots, and bargained on everything I could to make it happen. It took a lot of sacrifice to make this trip happen but it was worth it.

7. **What's the number one piece of advice you recommend to someone who is budgeting for their first travel experience?**

I would first ask yourself, "What's the purpose of your journey? What do you want to achieve and how far are you willing to go to make your dreams come true." Once you have your answers, money, time, and budget will fall into place with your choices and how passionate you are about making it happen. Because, I've learned that if you really want something in life, you'll do anything to make it happen.

8. What's new and what do you have planned for 2019?

As a YouTuber, "social media influencer," and digital content creator, every few months my approach to capturing an adventure and sharing it with the world changes, so it's impossible for me to say what'll be new when you read this. However, I know I will continue to create epic inspirational videos, vlogs, and posts about traveling. Future destinations include traversing by motorcycle south to north in Africa, and from East Russia to Western Europe. I hope you'll follow along for the adventure while creating your own.

INTERVIEW WITH
ALEXA MEISLER
BREAK INTO TRAVEL WRITING

Alexa is a truly inspirational woman with a serious knack for writing. Through her successful Facebook Group "The Aspiring Travel Writer", she's helped inspire thousands of wanderlusters to fulfill their dreams of travel writing. She also has a regular podcast with all the tips and tricks that's a MUST to listen to. We're so honored to have the opportunity to interview her. Read on!

1. **We recommend your podcast as a must-listen for aspiring travel writers. What made you start the podcast?**

   I chose to start the podcast, because I wanted to talk about and share what I learned as a freelance travel journalist turned travel blogger. I know so many have a dream of traveling more and don't quite know how to make it happen. I share how to get started as a writer or blogger so you can travel more for much less or even free. My goal is to share and teach anyone with a passion for travel and a desire to share their story how to become a travel writer or blogger.

2. **How would you make the most of a travel convention such as the LA Travel and Adventure show (we recommend this**

convention in the book).

I've actually done several podcasts on LA Travel and Adventure show. It's an amazing opportunity to learn about locations all over the world and talk with experts.

As a travel writer or blogger, I recommend attending the media preview, bring lots of cards to provide to the destinations and know in advance which locations you want to talk with.

As a traveler, I recommend wearing very comfortable shoes and arriving early, because it gets more crowded as the day goes on. Take time to talk with as many exhibitors as you can. Learn more about locations close to home as well as one's you may never have heard of. Ask about the best time to visit a location, specifically when the weather is nice but not high season, so you can find the best deals for hotels and airfare.

3. **How did you get into travel blogging?**

I started as a freelance staff writer for Portland Family Magazine. From there I went on to write for many additional outlets including Northwest Magazine, Healing Lifestyles and Spas, Oregon.com and Examiner.com. I started the blog so I had more control over what I wrote about and what media trips I accepted.

4. **Are there any challenges traveling and being gluten-free?**

It's getting easier and easier to travel with a gluten allergy. Some locations are very easy to travel to such as Mexico and I also find Western Europe very easy. There are more and more gluten free-options, even bread in many places. The biggest challenge is a language barrier, so I always write down how to say "I'm gluten-free" in the language of the country I am visiting and carry it with me so I can show it to a server.

5. **What are your favorite destinations to travel to?**

My favorite city in the world is Paris. I also love Lviv, Ukraine, Cebu, Philippines, Guadalajara, Mexico, 1000 Islands, New York and every inch of Ireland.

6. **What are your plans for 2019 and where are you off to next?**

I'm off to Loreto, Mexico and London, England next. I've also got a trip to San Juan Del Sur, Nicaragua planned for this spring. It also looks like I'll be heading to Germany, Latvia and Switzerland this summer. After that, who knows!

7. **Where can readers find you?**

They can find me at 52 Perfect Days, a travel website sharing how to spend a perfect day in locations around the world and at the Break Into Travel Writing Podcast, which is a resource that teaches aspiring travel writers and bloggers how to jumpstart their writing career and travel around the world.

National Bucket List Day

LIVE YOUR BEST LIFE EVERY
STEP OF THE WAY.

JOIN THE MOVEMENT
#NATIONALBUCKETLISTDAY

WWW.NATIONALBUCKETLISTDAY.COM

21

MAY
2019

About the Author

Kaila and Kiki are avid travel and food writers based in Los Angeles, CA. Through their shared passion for music and adventure, they previously toured the world in an all Asian-American female rock band and developed an undying love for travel.

Kaila's award-winning work has been featured in media outlets such as VICE, Fodor's, SkyScanner, and The Matador Network. Kiki discovered her love for travel as a professional touring musician, who shared the stage with acts such as Taylor Swift, Usher, and more. Both Kaila and Kiki have also been featured on FOX News as TV travel experts, sharing their knowledge about travel hacks, tricks, and tips with their viewers.

For more information on Kaila and Kiki's travel story, check out www.30daytravel.com.

You can connect with me on:

🔗 http://www.30daytravel.com

Subscribe to my newsletter:

✉ https://www.nylonpink.tv/printables/

38127312R00149

Made in the USA
Middletown, DE
05 March 2019